Here Is
ALASKA

Here Is
ALASKA

New Revised Edition

EVELYN STEFANSSON

CHARLES SCRIBNER'S SONS

NEW YORK

1 3 5 7 9 11 13 15 17 19 H/C 20 18 16 14 12 10 8 6 4 2
Printed in the United States of America
Library of Congress Catalog Card Number 72–11228
SBN 684-13253-2 (RB)

ILLUSTRATION ACKNOWLEDGMENTS

Grateful acknowledgment is made for permission to use the following:

PHOTOGRAPHS: pp. 42, 94, 146, courtesy of Alaska Airlines; pp. 160–161, courtesy Alaska Coastal Airways; pp. 4, 7, 8, 9, 12, 16, courtesy of Alyeska Pipeline Service Company; pp. 115, 152, courtesy of The American Museum of Natural History; pp. 133, 134, 136–137, by Ted Bank II, courtesy of Monkmeyer Press Photo Service; p. 88, courtesy of Bechtel Corporation; p. 89, courtesy of Bertrand-Marignane; p. 164, courtesy of Alberta Utt Falk; p. 22, courtesy of General Dynamics Corporation; p. 59, courtesy of Richard Harrington; pp. 25, 150, by Victor Heusser, courtesy of Geophysical Institute, University of Alaska; p. 126, courtesy of Kodiak Historical Society; pp. 40, 41, courtesy of Dorothe Livingston; p. 52 (bottom), courtesy of Lomen Bros.; pp. 20, 34, 50–51, 53, 55, 58, 60, 65, 66, 70, 71, 91, 96–97, 112–113, 154–155, 156–157, courtesy of Frederick Machetanz; p. 163, by NARL, courtesy of John Schindler; p. 52 (top), courtesy of The National Museum, Copenhagen; pp. 31, 81, 83, 109, courtesy of Pan American World Airways; pp. 28, 36, 38, 39, 107, 125, courtesy of State of Alaska, Department of Economic Development; titlepage and pp. 11, 13, 24, 26, 33, 37, 45, 57, 63, 68, 74, 76, 77, 78, 87, 93, 100, 102, 103, 104, 105, 106, 119, 123, 124, 127, 140, 141, 148, 149, 165, 167, 170, by Evelyn Stefansson Nef; p. 21, courtesy of Judge Thomas Stewart; pp. 23, 84–85, 86, courtesy of Western Electric. MAPS: pp. 2–3, by Van English; p. 14, by Jerry Thorpe. SCHEMATIC DRAWING: p. 49, courtesy of Smithsonian Institution.

ACKNOWLEDGMENTS

Traditionally Alaskans have always been friendly and hospitable. Happily most of them are still willing to share food, shelter, information, transportation, and their best photographs with visiting writers. My warm collective thanks go to all who were kind on my 1971 trip. Of those who were generous above and beyond even the high Alaskan norm I would like to thank particularly

in Anchorage, Sara and Fred Machetanz (the idea for this book was Fred's); Kay Fanning; Mr. and Mrs. Robert Atwood; Walter Hickel; and Prof. and Mrs. Charles Konigsburg;

in Fairbanks at the University, T. Neil Davis; Prof. and Mrs. William Hunt; Michael Krauss; and John Teal;

for a trip along the proposed pipeline route, Tim Bradner of BP Alaska; Tom Brennan of the Atlantic Richfield Company; the Alyeska Pipeline Service Company; and Prof. of Wildlife Management Robert Weedon who accompanied us;

in Juneau, Judge and Mrs. Thomas B. Stewart and Prof. and Mrs. George Rogers;

in Sitka, Margaret Fedoroff and Jessie Geeslin;

in Kodiak, Ella Mae Warren;

at Point Barrow, Mr. and Mrs. Tom Brower; Dorothe Livingston; at the Naval Arctic Research Laboratory, Max Brewer, former director; John Schindler, present director; and Don Sanders;

on the sea ice north of Barrow, Floyd Durham and Joeb Woods who saved my life when I fell through the sea ice at an Eskimo whaling camp;

in Washington, D. C., Keith Hay; Guy Martin, assistant to the late Congressman Nick Begich; Terry Scanlin and Darlene Hickey for secretarial help; and most of all Senator Ernest Gruening who continues to work dynamically and inspire all who want to learn more about Alaska and those who need a hero.

For Mary and Anne

Contents

List of
Illustrations

Crossroads

ALASKA IS A CHAMPION, Alaska is a record breaker, a land of surprises, contrasts, paradox and superlatives, a place of incredible beauty and unimaginable wealth. Alaska is our largest state with the smallest population. Alaska has the highest mountain in North America and the largest single source of furs in the world. She has the most valuable fisheries of any state, the coldest winters, potentially the richest oil fields, the highest wages, fewest social distinctions, and more men than women.

To balance that rosy picture we turn and discover its other, darker side. Continuing in the record-breaking tradition, we find Alaska has the highest cost of living of any state, the highest rates of accident, alcoholism, unemployment and suicide, the worst housing, and the most shaming poverty. Frame the picture with a disturbing statistic—fifty-six of every hundred workers in Alaska are government employees.

But the trouble with Alaska is that she is not at all like a picture. She is far more like a living child. A young, beautiful, rich, spirited, healthy child, capable of learning all things, good and bad. Miraculously growing, she captures hearts with her blind innocence and beauty and is infuriating in her experimental wickedness. Alaska can grow up to be anything she wants to be, but she has come suddenly and with little preparation to a dangerous crossroads. Perhaps adolescence with its terrible-wonderful turmoil is a better image with which to describe what the country is experiencing today, physically, politically, and morally.

The coming of age of Alaska's native peoples and the discovery of new, important oil and gas riches are two challenging events in the state's recent history. The manner in which these two problems are resolved will determine her future.

Like a loving, worried parent I'm standing by, nervously remembering that a burnt child's brother doesn't fear the fire and that mistakes are a necessary, wholesome part of the growing-up process. May at least the majority of the crucial decisions made in the coming year be the right ones for Alaska.

Chateau Castel Novel
Varetz, France
August 18, 1972

Here Is
ALASKA

Barrow
Wainwright
70°
CHUKCHI SEA
U.S.S.R.
Point Hope
Colville River
Umiat
BROOKS
Noatak River
Noatak
Anaktuvu Pass
Kotzebue
Kobuk R.
Kobuk
ARCTIC CIRCLE
BERING STRAIT
Little Diomede I.
Big Diomede I.
INTERNATIONAL DATE LINE
King I.
SEWARD PENINSULA
Nome
St. Lawrence I.
NORTON SOUND
Unalakleet
St. Michael
YUKON RIVER
Tanana
Ruby
170°
BERING SEA
Mt. McKinley
Kuskokwim River
Mekoryuk
60°
Nunivak I.
Bethel
ALASKA
Matanusk
Eklutna
Anchorage
KENAI PENIN.
Seward
Iliamna Lake
Cook Inlet
Homer
58°
PRIBILOF IS.
St. George
BRISTOL BAY
ALASKA PENINSULA
Kodiak
Kodiak I.
160°
Unimak I.
Akutan I.
Dutch Harbor
Unalaska I.
ISLANDS
SHUMAGIN IS.
Simeonof I.
Attu I.
NEAR IS.

Prudhoe Bay

Herschel I.

MACKENZIE
RIVER

Here is
ALASKA

ON R.   Fort Yukon

College
Fairbanks

Tanana River

RANGE

Scale in Miles
50   0   100   200

V. English

CANADA

Whitehorse

Valdez

Mt. St. Elias

Cordova

ce William
Sound

GULF
of
ALASKA

Skagway
Haines

Mendenhall Glacier

Douglas   Juneau

ALEXANDER

Sitka   ARCHIPELAGO

Petersburg
Wrangell

Ketchikan
Metlakatla

Annette

140°

EUTIAN ISLANDS

ISLANDS OF
THE FOUR
MOUNTAINS

ISLANDS   ANDREANOF is.

Atka I.

Umnak
Nikolski

chitka I. 180°   0 MILES 150 170°

CHAPTER I

Oil Rush

IN 1968 OIL IN GREAT QUANTITY was discovered at Prudhoe Bay on the Arctic shore of the North Slope, and the state of Alaska will never be the same again. The international oil industry arrived in force and irreversible changes took place. Payment the following year of $900 million to the state for oil and gas leases not only balanced the budget of a poor state, it was enough to run it for four and a half years. The promise of future tax and royalty payments danced in Alaskan heads, and to many the principal problem seemed to be how to spend so much money. As the good news spread, optimists streamed into the state and the ever-present housing shortage became acute.

Booms were not new in Alaskan history. Gold rushes had peopled the state when it was still an infant territory, but in their wildest dreams Alaskans had not envisioned activity on this grand scale.

At first all precise information about the size of the oil

OPPOSITE: Summer on the North Slope dramatically changes the dry, frozen winter prairie into a scene of endless meltwater pools and small lakes. The oil-drilling rigs are conspicuous on the treeless horizon.

reserves was an industrial secret. Periodically, "reliable sources" announced figures which started at 10 billion barrels of oil and gradually increased to 50 billion, with square cubic feet of accompanying natural gas in the trillions.

Oil has been known to exist in northern North America since the eighteenth century, but the meaningful history of oil in Alaska began in July, 1957, when it was discovered in south central Alaska on Kenai Peninsula in quantities sufficient to exploit profitably. By 1969 five oil and nine natural gas fields were producing and the petroleum industry had become Alaska's most important cash crop. A pipeline was built to carry gas to nearby Anchorage and refineries constructed to produce the jet, diesel, and heating fuels that previously had to be imported. Plants appeared for producing ammonia and prilled urea and for liquifying natural gas to ship to Tokyo in refrigerated tankers. But the Cook Inlet-Kenai Peninsula oil and gas fields were small compared to the Prudhoe Bay discoveries.

As estimates of the size of the North Slope reserves grew, several oil companies combined and proposed building a hot oil pipeline, forty-eight inches in diameter, from Prudhoe Bay straight south for eight hundred miles across three mountain ranges to Valdez on Prince William Sound. From the deepwater ice-free port of Valdez, tankers would transport it to the northwest coast of the lower forty-eight states.

Many cities in Alaska suffered in the devastating 1964 earthquake, the worst in Alaska's history, but Valdez was virtually wiped out. Residents of the Cook Inlet–Kenai Peninsula area, where the oil industry was already flourishing, knew another side of the optimistic picture. Theirs included oil spills, dead wildlife, polluted waters, and ruined fisheries.

A second voice began to accompany the deliriously happy oil song of money, jobs, and future prosperity. It was that of the environmentalists reminding that the proposed pipeline crossed very difficult terrain: mountains, rivers (including the mighty Yukon), permafrost of infinite variety, and earthquake

An aerial view of the proposed terminal site of the trans-Alaska oil pipeline at Valdez, a year-round icefree port.

zones. The climatic conditions were also severe. Ecologists now asked embarrassing questions about what a hot oil pipeline, which the company proposed to bury, would do to the surrounding permafrost; about the fate of the migrating caribou and the Eskimos who depend on them for survival; about what would happen to the fisheries if an oil tanker should break apart in a storm. They pointed to the useless 470-mile-long Hickel Highway, a winter road to the North Slope, hastily built at great cost and barely finished before the summer sun turned it into a useless, muddy, deformed scar across Alaska's beautiful face.

War was declared between the oil companies and the conservationists. Alaska had never seen such drama, involving so many people, and so much money, even in the wildest days of the gold rushes. Every means offered by the modern news media was used by both sides to plead their cause: honest truth, semi-honest truth, exaggerated truth, and half-truth.

Alaskans were divided. Opinion ranged from those who saw in the oil development salvation for the state and the solution of all its problems, to the other extreme, those who viewed it as the gravest threat to the last unspoiled U.S. wilderness, not one acre of which should be despoiled The environ mentalists, many of them Alaskans who wished oil had never

In a Prudhoe Bay oil field caribou graze unconcernedly in sight of the operating drill rigs.

An archeological survey of the entire route of the 789-mile pipeline was recently completed.

been discovered in their state, pledged their efforts to prevent its being exploited. Time has educated both sides and it now seems clear to a growing number that it is possible to both develop and conserve and to do so at the same time.

The environmentalists must be credited with educating the public and the oil companies. The oil companies must be credited with a commitment to cherish and preserve the environment. Public opinion is now so strong as to leave them no choice in the matter. Oil and pipeline companies have hired ecologists and scientists to tell them how to proceed in Arctic and tundra Alaska with minimum damage to the environment. They have taken into careful consideration, at great cost to themselves, the dangers of disturbing permafrost, vegetation, wildlife, river beds, and archeological sites. They have studied the enormous literature, instituted many new studies at the

University of Alaska and elsewhere, and made reassuring promises about the care, caution, and precautions that will be taken at every step of the oil and gas development from searching, drilling, and production, to building and maintaining a pipeline and tanker shipments.

Meanwhile the U.S. Department of the Interior considered the wisdom of issuing a permit for construction of the pipeline. Three years and three months after receiving the pipeline proposal, on May 11, 1972, Secretary of the Interior Rogers Morton gave his official approval. Before doing so he and his department produced one of the most massive reports (even for a government department) in history.

As we go to press the way ahead is still not clear. Court suits brought by the environmentalists are delaying the construction of the pipeline, and Prudhoe Bay oil production has halted, no one knows for how long.

Confident that the legal tangles will soon be solved, Governor of Alaska William Egan in May, 1972, gave his assurance that the pipeline project "will be a model for the world as far as environmental safeguards are concerned, both as to the construction period and as to the steps which will be taken to insure environmental protection in the transporting of oil to American refineries."

One of the good results of the oil controversy was the relatively speedy settlement of the land claims of Alaskan natives. When we purchased Alaska from Russia in 1867 we agreed to respect the rights of the aborigines. There was much talk but little action in this area. By the time of the Prudhoe Bay discoveries the Alaskan natives, who began to organize on a large scale back in the 1960s, were ready for action. They threatened the oil companies with promises of numerous and lengthy land law suits, which could delay the exploitation of oil for years, and even started proceedings in some cases.

While the search for more oil reserves continued, the Alyeska Pipeline Company not unnaturally hesitated to invest the $4 billion needed to construct the line without having clear title to the land it crossed. I believe oil industry pressure was a major factor in getting a satisfactory Alaska Native Claims Settlement Act through Congress. (See page 30 for the details.) A formidable barrier to the building of the pipeline was thereby removed.

An important dividend of oil exploration in Alaska was the discovery of some twenty natural gas fields, usually but not always found in conjunction with oil. Drilling has reached below a depth of 13,500 feet in the Cook Inlet-Kenai Peninsula area. Here both onshore and offshore gas fields are supplying fuel to Anchorage and also producing the 47.5 billion cubic feet per year which are cooled, liquified, and shipped to Japan by tanker. Alaska gas is relatively pure, 99 percent methane, with very low air-polluting sulphur content. Canadian compa-

The oil field at Prudhoe Bay is a noisy place while drilling is in progress. The automated recorder registered a depth of 7,414.5 feet when this picture was taken.

A forty-foot section of pipe for the pipeline is guided into the Fairbanks pipeyard.

nies have already contracted for Prudhoe Bay gas, and a gas pipeline is planned eastward into Arctic Canada, and then southeastward, following the giant Mackenzie River until it meets existing gas pipelines.

In March, 1971, the Canadian government through diplomatic channels suggested to the U.S. government and public that an oil pipeline following the Mackenzie River route to Edmonton should be substituted for the trans-Alaska pipeline. The Canadians said it would be cheaper and safer from an environmental point of view.

Noting that the 1,700-mile Mackenzie Valley route, although longer than the Alyeska route, crosses no earthquake zones and requires no transshipment by oil tanker, ecologically-minded opponents of the Alaska route agreed. They believe that all North Slope oil should be brought south through Canada's Northwest Territories and Prairie Provinces, using the same river valley route as the planned Canadian gas pipeline. This would bring oil directly to midwestern United States from where it could be distributed more efficiently. The Friends of the Earth, the Wilderness Society, and the Environmental Defense Fund have joined forces and filed suit for a permanent injunction against the building of the Alaska pipeline. They claim insufficient consideration has been given the Canadian route. They have lost the first legal battle but intend to appeal. Secretary of the Interior Morton, in defending the Alyeska route, stated that for national security reasons the pipeline should be on U.S. soil and exclusively for U.S. use. He

Professor Robert B. Weeden of the University of Alaska's Department of Wildlife and Fisheries poses in the forty-eight-inch diameter pipeline pipe "for scale."

also pointed out that gas and oil cannot be transported through the same pipeline or even share the same route. Oil is hot, 160° F., when it emerges from depths of eight to nine thousand feet at Prudhoe Bay, and may even increase in temperature as it flows through pipe. Gas can be cooled until liquid and transported at below freezing temperatures. A gas pipeline can

Environmentalists advocate a pipeline route from Prudhoe Bay through Canada via the Mackenzie Valley because it requires no oil shipment by tanker. The Prudhoe Bay-Valdez route is shorter and entirely on U.S. territory but tankers are a necessary part of its system.

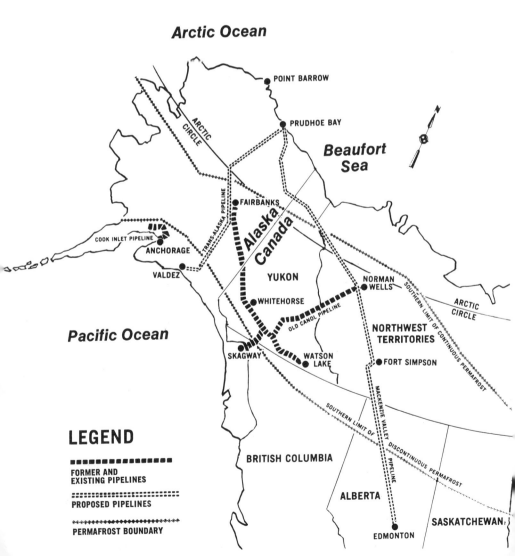

therefore be buried in the permafrost without damaging it, while a hot oil pipeline must be elevated to prevent deformation of the permafrost. The pipeline company which earlier proposed to bury the pipeline, after studying the difficulties, came to the conclusion that about half of the eight-hundred-mile line would have to be built above ground because of permafrost.

As its name implies, permafrost is perpetually frozen ground, which varies in thickness from a few inches to the 1,330 feet found south of Barrow. It is composed of frozen earth, ice, rock, or gravel, or any combination of those materials. Between the top of the permafrost and the vegetation cover above it is an area known as the *active layer*, which unlike the permafrost thaws and freezes with the seasons. Scientists usually divide permafrost into three zones: *continuous permafrost*, where all the ground below the active layer is always frozen; *discontinuous permafrost*, where some ground is and some isn't frozen; and *sporadic permafrost*, ground which contains islands of frozen earth. Vegetation that grows above permafrost acts as a kind of heavy quilt that prevents the action of the sun from penetrating downward. After more than a half century of permafrost engineering research we know that the best method of coping with it is to *keep it frozen*, whether one is building a road, airfield, pipeline, or log cabin.

In permafrost land the turning wheels of a heavy vehicle will kill the fragile vegetation it crosses. When the vegetation dies and turns brown it begins to absorb the heat of the sun's rays instead of deflecting them as living vegetation does. The absorbed heat thaws the surrounding earth, which becomes a muddy and unstable area that slowly and continuously enlarges, like a giant oozing wound. Trees growing in permafrost areas have shallow roots that grow out horizontally in the narrow active layer. When a chain saw cuts a path into such a forested area, the sun thaws the path, releasing the previously frozen roots. The wind soon topples these trees the way hail

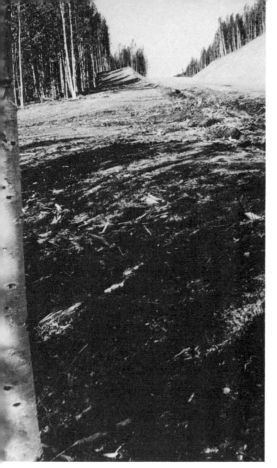

LEFT: The highway between Livengood and the Yukon River after construction in June, 1970. RIGHT: In August of the same year after special seeding and fertilizing. This grass will hold the soil until natural vegetation takes over.

levels a field of ripe grain. Once the blanket cover of impermeable vegetation is disturbed, the deformation of the exposed landscape is certain unless measures are taken to forestall the inexorable process. Among the many studies made by the oil companies is one to test various types of fast-growing grass seeds to determine which is best to plant in areas disturbed by their activities. The results so far are promising.

In the summer of 1969 one of the Prudhoe Bay oil companies sent its 1,005-foot-long tanker *Manhattan*, the largest ship ever to penetrate Arctic waters, on a much-publicized Northwest Passage voyage designed to test the feasibility of bringing out oil directly from the North Slope by ship. Despite heroic and glowing bulletins issued regularly during the course of the voyage it was found to be impractical. The *Manhattan* reached Prudhoe Bay and Point Barrow, but several times it was caught fast in the pack ice and freed only with the help of U.S. and Canadian icebreakers. The tanker was damaged but fortunately was carrying no oil on its trial run. The voyage was one of several costly errors made in the early excitement of the oil discovery period. A safer method of transport, immune from ice and storm damage, would be a fleet of nuclear-powered submarine tankers. Submarines can function below the pack ice with ease and relative safety both summer and winter since wave action is not transmitted downward. The successful polar journeys of the U.S. Navy's *Nautilus*, *Skate*, and *Seadragon* confirm this. The company that built these nuclear-powered submarines for the navy has proposed to build a fleet of five submarine oil tankers, but their proposal has not been accepted to date. The *Manhattan* fiasco turned transport thinking back to the pipeline.

The Alyeska Company pipeline, when it is finally built, will not be the first oil pipeline in Alaska. During World War II the U.S. Army Corps of Engineers built a pipeline entirely above ground from the Canadian Norman Wells oil fields to Skagway, Watson Lake, and Fairbanks. It was the first large-scale project of its kind and introduced thousands of workers to the north country's muskeg, tundra, and permafrost. Sixteen hundred miles of pipe were laid over the most difficult kind of northern terrain without disaster. The pipe was of far smaller diameter than the proposed forty-eight-inch Alyeska line, only four and six inches in diameter. When the war and emergency were over, the Canol (for Canadian oil) project was dismantled.

It is already clear that those who foresaw in the oil industry a solution to Alaska's high unemployment rate will be disappointed. Once established and functioning, after the initial search and the discovery and establishment of wells, storage facilities, and processing plants are over, the oil industry is highly automated and employs relatively few people. Those few are usually workers with highly trained skills that Alaskans, especially natives, as a rule lack. Most of the specialists brought into Alaska will leave when their jobs are finished and be sent on to the next promising oil area. Alaska natives may share in the oil royalties but they will find few permanent oil-connected jobs.

Although the end is in sight, Alaska's oil war continues. Her neighbor to the east, Canada, has also been searching for and finding oil in promising quantities. The Canadian government plans the building of an all-year road along the Mackenzie River route to aid and encourage development. If one thinks of the Arctic Ocean as a Mediterranean Sea, with the same oil potential as the old Mediterranean, it is easy to prophesy that both the Canadian and Alaska pipelines will be built to handle the immense quantities of oil and gas that will be produced on Arctic shores and shipped to the fuel-hungry industrial centers of the south.

CHAPTER II

Forty-ninth
State

ON THE NIGHT of June 30, 1958, the U.S. Senate, by a vote of sixty-four to twenty, touched off a gigantic celebration that extended from Alaska's mild, wooded, southeastern shore to its northernmost permafrosted tip, Point Barrow. Huge bonfires had been prepared, and the moment word was received they were kindled by jubilant crowds. Bands, speeches, fireworks, parades, shouting and dancing in the streets were all part of joyous demonstrations that lasted through the night and well into the day. For the bill the Senate had passed at 8:02 P.M. assured the admission of the Territory of Alaska into the Union as our forty-ninth state. On August 26, in the heaviest election turnout in Alaska's history, her people voted five to one in favor of statehood.

Alaska was ready for this moment! Three years before she had adopted the Tennessee Plan, a program drawn up and first applied in 1796 by the vigorous pioneers of the Territory of Tennessee in *their* fight for statehood. The first item called for by the plan was a constitutional convention. In September, 1955, therefore, Alaska's Territorial Legislature elected fifty-five convention delegates, and the following November they gathered on the campus of the University of Alaska to draft a constitution.

Continuing according to the Tennessee Plan, the conven-

The first newspapers announcing statehood.

tion provided for the immediate election of two "senators" and a "representative" from Alaska to go to Washington. These phantom legislators, who had no legal status in Congress, were charged with going to the capitol to lobby for Alaskan statehood. Former Governor Ernest Gruening was one senator-elect, and William A. Egan, of Valdez, president of the constitutional convention, the other. Ralph J. Rivers was the lone representative. Combining forces with Alaska's beloved congressional delegate, E. L. Bartlett, these well-informed, able men brought to the attention of Washington and the nation reasons why Alaska should become a state. In the time between his governorship and his "senatorship," Gruening had written a penetrating political history of the Territory, called *The State of Alaska*, setting forth past misgovernment, present problems, and the arguments favoring statehood. Young Mike Stepovich, the first Alaska-born governor, had also helped the fight; so too had the secretary of the interior, Fred Seaton, the first man in his position to interest himself deeply in Alaska and her problems.

To the majority of Alaskans, alerted and tense, word of statehood arriving by radio and telephone brought news of victory—a battle won. Statehood meant an end of colonialism and "taxation-without-representation." In the past, while Delegate Bartlett might make speeches in the halls of Congress, he had no vote, despite the payment of federal income taxes by his constituents. Statehood meant at last the possibility of controlling the one-way traffic in the largely absentee-owned fishing and mining industries. Almost since the purchase of Alaska in 1867, these industries had drained her riches. Money, equipment, even labor, came from outside and profits went outside, leaving Alaska depleted in natural and financial resources. But perhaps the most important reaction to statehood for Alaskans was a happy feeling of equality with all other U.S. citizens—a coming of age.

A portion of the rich dowry Alaska brought to her union with the United States was her strategic position. On the north

The author meets Governor William Egan in his Juneau office.

ABOVE: *The U.S.S.* Nautilus *welcomed home to Groton, Connecticut. PANOPOS (on signs) stands for "Pacific Atlantic North Pole."*

RIGHT: *From the air, a typical DEW Line station's cluster of buildings and equipment surrounding the dome-shaped housing of the main search antenna.*

Alaska faces the Arctic Sea, newest aerial and submarine crossroads of the world; to the west across Bering Sea and Strait lies the Soviet Union. Two huge, costly defense alarm systems now guard these shores. One is the DEW Line, or Distant Early Warning radar screen, which starts in the Canadian Arctic and girdles the North American mainland westward to Alaska. Here it continues along the northern and western shores to and through the Aleutian Islands. The second defense installation is White Alice, a complicated communications system using huge twin antennas, sixty feet high, set up at stations about two hundred miles apart. However bothersome the sun spots or stormy the weather, whatever the hour of day or night, White Alice provides certain communication

between outposts and mainland in an area where radio black-
outs occur at unexpected intervals and may last a fortnight.
White Alice, the latest in tropospheric electronics when it was
completed in the mid-fifties, still stands guard from villages
where Eskimos hunt whales from skin-covered umiaks.

Since 1930 Alaska's population has been growing. Anchorage and Fairbanks are now booming cities, complete with tall
buildings, modern housing developments, motels, parking meters, and traffic problems. The state's rich resources are being
developed, some of them for the first time. Fishing and mining, long the most important industries, have new competition
from the defense industry, pulp manufacturing, and most recently petroleum. The discovery in 1957 of Alaska's first rich
commercial oil fields just outside Anchorage started an oil-

A pulp mill at Ketchikan.

The aurora borealis paints Alaska's skies with light and brilliant color.

Long summer days produce a rich cover of grasses, flowers, and shrubs.

leasing rush reminiscent of early Klondike days, which was accelerated by North Slope discoveries.

Alaska is our largest state, two and a quarter times the size of Texas. Her area, 586,400 square miles, increased the total square mileage of the United States to more than 3.5 million. Her islands and indented shores added more than 33,000 miles to U.S. coastlines. Her soils and mountains contain thirty-one of the thirty-three so-called strategic minerals, in addition to proven deposits of natural gas, fabulously rich oil lands, and possibilities of almost infinite hydroelectric power. The tallest mountain in the state, 20,320-foot Mount McKinley, is the highest in North America. Alaska is our only state extending into the Eastern Hemisphere, for the Aleutian Islands reach beyond the 180th meridian to about 170° east longitude. This is a big, tall, wide, rich record-breaking state!

Though she lacks numbers, Alaska's population is younger and more energetic than that of other states. The average Alaskan is seven years younger than the average citizen in the rest of the United States. This youthfulness is responsible for

Alaska having the highest birth rate and lowest death rate of any state. In 1970 her population numbered 302,647, of which 50,654 were Eskimos, Aleuts, and forest Indians. The military population remains steady at about 33,000. Although once far more numerous than they are today, Alaska's natives are now surviving, but they are poorer and their health is worse than formerly.

Among all peoples whose ancestors were never exposed to the disease, tuberculosis is one of the greatest killers. Soon after the white man's coming to Alaska, TB began to claim Eskimo and Indian lives and continued to do so in terrifying numbers. Now at last the disease has been curbed, if not stopped, and the outlook for control is brighter, thanks to a vigorous U.S. Public Health Service program and the cooperative Alaska Health Department.

Two things Alaska needs most to assure and secure a prosperous future are settlers and investment capital. She needs the capital in order to produce cement from her limestone; lumber, pulp, and paper from her forests; salmon and shrimp from local waters; fuels from her oil and gas reserves; and food from her fertile lands. Her rich resources can easily support a greatly expanded population.

Chilkat Indians, part of the Tlingit family, are famous for their valuable blankets which predate so-called modern art.

CHAPTER III

The Natives
Come of Age

THE SAD OLD STORY of primitive man's first encounters with so-called civilized man was acted out in Alaska just as in other states and parts of the world, except that it happened more recently in Alaska. Friendly, curious, and trust-ing, until taught differently, Alaskan natives were easy prey for the Russians, who killed many and virtually enslaved others in the interest of the fur trade. After the Purchase it was our turn and we decimated them too, albeit unintentionally, through the biological warfare of measles and tuberculosis. This was followed by an equally disastrous kind of sociological warfare resulting in native poverty, malnutrition, and more recently, loss of self-esteem, alcoholism, and suicide.

At first the natives were the dominant people and white invaders a minority, usually in need of something—food, cloth-ing, furs, information, or transportation. It is one more of history's ironies that these roles are now reversed. Today the white man and his ways prevail and the natives are the minority. The white man is rich and the native is poor. The white man is healthy and the native is sick, with the white man's diseases. The white man is educated, but 60 percent of the natives have less than an eighth grade education, and their little learning is badly, sometimes cruelly, taught and, until very recently, always in a foreign language, English. Crowded into poor villages and urban slums, deprived of their former hunting grounds by state, federal, and big business land take-overs, they suffer from what is fashionably called "culture shock," a phrase which gives little idea of their miserable lot. They have the most squalid housing in the entire United States. Necessity has forced their dependence on white man's food, fuel, and shelter, all of which cost money. But there are few or no jobs in the little villages, so a native must leave his family for a larger village or a city. There he must find a job to earn the money to buy the goods the white man has taught him—indeed, forced him—to need. Coupled with Alaska's notorious high cost of living (it costs 250 percent more to build a house at Point Barrow than in Seattle), it is small wonder that Alaskan natives are troubled, frustrated, and, for the first time in this writer's experience, hostile. Professor George Rogers of the University of Alaska coined an unforgettable phrase of profound insight which sums up the lot of Alaska's natives when he wrote that they lived in a "fragmented ghetto."

As U.S. citizens Alaskan natives are entitled to schooling (indeed the law insists on it), certain welfare and health ser-vices, social security, and other familiar benefits. Actually, spread out over an immense and often harsh territory, those farthest from the city administrative centers sometimes receive a fraction of their due and sometimes none at all.

At long last a turn has been made on this grim road. It is the Alaska Native Claims Settlement Act, which was passed by Congress and signed into law by President Nixon on December 18, 1971. One hundred and four years after the Purchase, the land claims of Alaska's original inhabitants have finally been appropriately recognized—not to everyone's de-light, to be sure, but on the whole a better, fairer arrangement than many had hoped for.

The new law affects the life of all fifty thousand Eskimos, Indians, and Aleuts in the state. It enables them to eventually select and own 40 million acres of land and calls for $962.5

million in federal appropriations and mineral royalties from oil production to be paid to them. This will be accomplished through the formation of 200 village corporations and 12 larger regional corporations in which every native will be able to participate. The first widespread result of the act is a giant enrollment project, the largest of its kind ever attempted by the United States. By the end of 1973 every native will have his name listed on a Bureau of Indian Affairs roll even if he has moved from the state. The act defines a native as any U.S. citizen of one quarter or more Alaskan Indian, Eskimo, or Aleut blood or combination thereof.

There is much lively discussion and speculation about what changes for better or worse will result from the act. Many

An Eskimo family.

natives hope it will not change their actual way of life, especially those engaged in subsistence hunting. Others believe it
will permit villages to become self-supporting units once more.
Some see a political and financial power emerging which will
command improved housing, health measures, education,
technical training, and better employment possibilities. New
ways of thinking will be required; the very idea of *owning* land
would be strange, for instance, to a primitive Eskimo. The idea
of Indians cooperating with traditional enemies—the Eskimos
—might seem impossible to an old-timer but it is being done.
The circumstances which finally brought about the Land Settlement made the old modes of operation obsolete. One ele-
ment in the success was a new understanding of how to operate
in a white man's world. Where the natives lacked technical
knowledge, say in the law, they hired lawyers and called in
experts and advisers to guide them. Thus they were able to
accomplish in a decade what they had previously been unable
to do in a century.

The most important part of the activity ending in the
Settlement was the establishment in 1966 of the Alaska Feder-
ation of Natives, which was organized specifically for the purpose of obtaining a land settlement. All through the 1960s
twenty-four separate native groups had been formed, from the
northernmost Eskimos to the southernmost Indians and including the westernmost Aleuts. Despite differences and rival-
ries, ancient and modern, for the first time in history these
people were consolidated into one authoritative voice speaking
for *all* the natives of Alaska.

Before the AFN could come into being groundwork had
to be laid. The American Association of Indian Affairs began
to operate in Alaska and helped two pioneering events take
place: the establishment in 1961 of *Inupiat Paitot* (People's
Heritage), the first native Eskimo organization, and the following year the birth of the *Tundra Times*, the first Alaskan
newspaper dedicated to native problems. Howard Rock, an

Howard Rock, the influential and universally admired Eskimo editor of the Tundra Times.

Eskimo, directed the former and edited the latter. He has become a respected, influential writer and spokesman for the native point of view. As an editor he gathers information from many sources, provides a forum for differing opinions, and effectively champions native rights.

The 1970 census counted 50,654 natives in Alaska. Fifty-two percent (27,797) of them are Eskimo, 14 percent (6,581) are Aleut, and 34 percent (16,276) Indian. In the old days the Tlingit Indians who live in the southeastern part of Alaska had a wealthy, aristocratic society which included slavery, a considerable unwritten literature, and the potlatch.

The potlatch was a public celebration where, to the accompaniment of singing, dancing, dramatic recitations, and feasting, a man would give away rich gifts. Here a new totem pole would be dedicated, marriages celebrated, claims and proclamations announced, and fine clothes displayed. At first glance, it would seem to be a scheme for pauperization, for a chief

might give away most of his possessions, including huge dug-
out canoes and valuable Chilkat blankets. But a careful tally
was kept of all presents and rigid etiquette demanded that all
gifts be returned with interest, which might run as high as 100
percent. In effect, the potlatch was a banking system, and a
form of insurance, investment, social security, and credit circu-
lation. If a man died, the gift was owed to his heirs. To avoid
payment was unthinkable. Traditionally, all gifts were supposed to be of the finest workmanship, made from the best
materials. So the potlatch stimulated every form of art to its
highest pitch, whether in weaving of mats, baskets, and blankets, or the carving of jewelry, gift boxes, canoes, or totem
poles.

Totem poles, usually placed at the entrance to a man's
house, commemorated a special event or, through animal sym-
bols, the family totem, or family tree. Many of the surviving
poles in Alaska have been preserved, carefully restored, or
reproduced. Fine examples may be seen at Sitka National
Monument Park, at Saxman Park outside Ketchikan, at the
Juneau Museum, and elsewhere. These great works of native
art, once ignored and permitted to decay, are now widely
appreciated. During the tourist season, they are among the
most photographed items in the land.

In addition to the Tlingits, Alaska's panhandle has two
other Indian groups: Tsimshians and Haidas. The prosperous
Tsimshians, who live mostly at Metlakatla, and the Haidas,
whose fathers migrated from British Columbia about four or
five hundred years ago, are small segments of large tribes still
living in Canada. Athapascan Indians, the largest single group
of Indians in North America, live in the interior and south
central part of Alaska. The Eyak Indians, who controlled the
copper trade and whose central point was at Cordova, have

OPPOSITE: *Chief Shake was a famous leader of the Tlingit Indians.*

now practically disappeared, through death and absorption by other groups.

Little remains of the old Indian cultures. The sons of great warriors are now the poorest people in the state. They work in canneries and pulp mills, or for shipping and airline companies. Most of their ancient, highly developed craft skills have been forgotten, but a few have been revived for souvenir-hungry visitors to Alaska. Since 1966, when the Alaska State Council on the Arts was formed, a revival on a higher artistic level has started. The council supports every kind of art, artist, and art organization with money and opportunity. They cooperate with the State Museum, the Tlingit-Haida Council, the Alaska Native Brotherhood, and others trying to save and support native arts and crafts that are in danger of dying. If dead they try resurrection, as with old Indian dances thought lost forever. Lessons are now available in Aleut basket making and Chilkat blanket weaving. Exhibitions are arranged so that beginning Eskimo carvers may see the best carving done in other villages. For the first time in years native interest is being kindled and linked with the highest artistic standards.

A Tlingit Indian basket made of spruce root.

At Sitka National Monument Park some of Alaska's finest totem poles have been preserved.

There is a renewal of interest in native crafts in Alaska. It includes the restoration and preservation of old totem poles and the making of new ones, some of them miniatures which will be sold as souvenirs.

The universally popular Eskimos are the largest group of native people in Alaska. After a long and almost disastrous population decline, they are increasing again. They are an able-bodied, good-humored, self-reliant, clever people, whose ancestors began to arrive in Alaska some fifteen thousand years ago. They live along the shores of the Arctic and Bering seas, as well as in the river deltas and in some cases up the river valleys, especially along the Colville, Noatak, Kobuk, and Kuskokwim rivers. They have always been a hunting people, following the fish and game animals with the seasons, but usually remaining in one general area. They hunted caribou, mountain sheep, and moose on the land; polar bear, seal, walrus, and whale at sea. Except for big city dwellers, most village Eskimos still derive at least part of their living from the same animals hunted by their ancestors.

To some extent the Eskimos have always been fishermen, particularly on the Bering coast. Through the influence of the Russian American Company, of the Hudson's Bay Company, and of the Free Traders (as the independent competitors of the great fur trading companies were called), they became fur trappers.

North of the Arctic Circle the majority of the Eskimos lived, for at least part of the year, on or near the coast. On the great inland prairie the population is now sparse; only fifty or sixty years ago it was inhabited by ten or perhaps twenty times as many Eskimos as now. Then and earlier, coastal folk de-

Ivory carving is an important source of income to some of Alaska's most remote Eskimos.

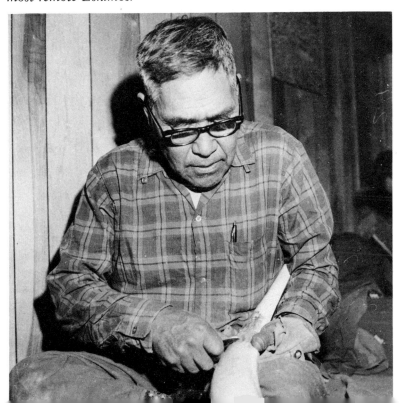

pended chiefly on seal and whale for food, and those of the interior lived on caribou, supplemented by birds, and fish from the inland lakes and rivers. In the mountains a comparatively few Eskimos lived mainly on sheep.

Seal, walrus, and whale oil provided coastal Eskimos with fuel and light. The inlanders used spruce, alder, and willow for fuel, and in their camps burned caribou tallow for light, or oil purchased from the coastal people in exchange for caribou hides and sheepskins. Once a year, most often in late winter, they would come down to the sea to hunt seals, to visit, and to trade.

Since their culture was so perfectly adapted to the climate of the Arctic, we tend to think of Eskimos as primarily an Arctic people. But more Eskimos live south of the latitude of Fairbanks than north of it.

The western and southern coasts of Alaska were in fairly

Eskimo women at a Point Barrow whaling camp.

Whaling is still an important food source for Point Barrow Eskimos.

close touch with the Russians and with other white men in the eighteenth century, and the interior similarly in the nineteenth. The northern coast had sporadic whalers a hundred years ago but no resident trader until Charles D. Brower settled at Barrow in 1885 and established his famous trading post. Generally throughout Alaska, missionaries followed close on the heels of the traders.

The whalers and traders needed fresh meat for food and to ward off the dreaded scurvy. They had never heard of vitamins, but sea captains knew if they had fresh meat they and their crews would remain in good health. So they offered lures of every sort to get the Eskimos to hunt for them.

Soon after the first contact between the two peoples, Alaskan natives began to die in great numbers from diseases brought in by the whites. This was no doubt so throughout all of Alaska, but we know the story best from the Eskimos. The

Muktuk *is a food delicacy to sea-mammal–hunting Eskimos.*

deadliness of the illnesses was due to their newness. No Eskimos had ever been exposed to them; therefore none had a natural immunity.

It is commonly believed that the worst killer that ever attacked the natives of the New World was smallpox. But insofar as we know the history of Alaska, the deadliest scourge was measles. There was an epidemic around the turn of the century which killed not less than one quarter of the people in any village we know about. This epidemic, according to a report we believe authentic, killed nearly 99 percent in one village, the only survivor being a girl of about six.

The second epidemic, a few years later, may have killed from 10 to 20 percent, the third killed only a few, and now the danger of measles to the Eskimos is not much greater than to us. Those who survived the first and second epidemics had an immunity against measles. Similar death rates from measles have been reported from tropical islands of the Pacific. Indeed a high mortality rate has been reported wherever measles had been previously unknown.

After measles, tuberculosis became the deadliest Eskimo

disease and held the lead for decades. The U.S. Public Health Service is responsible for all native Alaskan medical needs. Since 1951 they have made great strides through education, new drugs like Isoniazid (INH), and additional hospitals in lowering the death rate from tuberculosis. Few natives *die* of TB now, thanks to chemotherapy, but the number of new cases is still increasing. The terrible fact remains that 90 percent of Alaska's natives register TB positive in a tuberculin test —their bodies harbor the germs. The state provides free tests and free INH to prevent clinical cases from developing. It is no surprise that Alaska has the highest TB rate of all fifty states. Some think Eskimos always had tuberculosis but that it was kept in check by their wholesome food and old way of life. Others think, and this is the majority view, that Eskimos never had tuberculosis until it was introduced in historic times.

Under their "primitive" way of life Eskimos were free of many diseases which plague the white man. Apparently they formerly never had tooth decay, cancer, scurvy, or beriberi. As they shifted to the white man's way of life they acquired his diseases too, and now Eskimo teeth are as badly decayed as ours, the cancer rate is increasing, and alcoholism, mental illness, and suicide have become grave problems.

One of the few genuine benefits the whites brought to the Eskimos was the reduction of the death rate at childbirth for both mothers and children. Among primitive Eskimos it was not permissible for anyone to be present when a child was being born. The most custom permitted was that a woman's mother might be outside the house, shouting advice in to her daughter. In some areas, even this was taboo. But the Eskimos had one advantage, even in childbirth cases; the bacteria which cause infection were rare or absent. In the Arctic and sub-Arctic, almost every wound was formerly a clean wound. Despite great improvements the native infant mortality rate is twice that of the whites, and under the age of one year it is twelve times as high.

The Eskimos and Indians of Alaska used to be wards of the government. They had no rights of citizenship, but the government was pledged to look after their welfare. In 1924 an act of Congress provided that "all non-citizen Indians, born within the territorial limits of the United States, shall be citizens," and that the granting of citizenship shall not in any way affect the right of an Indian to tribal or other property. Some have contended that the Eskimos are not Indians and would not come under this law, but it has been ruled that the law does apply to them. It would be strange if the law did not, for biologically and anthropologically they are of the same race.

Until their contact with Europeans, when births began to be recorded by missionaries and school teachers, the Eskimos did not know how old they were, except in a vague way, and considered it unimportant. They did not reckon age by years but by terms like our "infant," "child," "youth," "adult." Primitive Eskimos counted by twenties, using both fingers and toes, where we use only the fingers; so that what corresponds to our hundred, ten times ten, is for them four hundred, twenty times twenty. Occasionally some Eskimo might tell you that it was not possible to count higher than four hundred, but if you pressed him he could usually devise an extension.

To measure distance the Eskimos had nothing like our miles, but reckoned a journey in fractions of a day. If it was more than two days, they usually spoke in number of days.

An idea, or at least a word, which they did not have was "year." They spoke of spring, summer, autumn, and winter, and they reckoned years either in winters or in summers.

They had months in the sense of moons and usually knew that there were thirteen in the complete cycle. But some of them would tell you that there were eight moons, nine moons, ten moons, according to what part of Alaska you were in, and then they would give the moonless period, which would be the summer, when the night was so bright that the moon could not be seen.

Eskimo children at Point Barrow.

One of the strangest ideas to an Eskimo was that of our cardinal, or compass, points. Their directional thinking was not governed by the sun, but rather by the shoreline, for most of them were coastal people. So their directional phrases are "up the coast," "down the coast," "inland," and "out to sea." This has been confusing to those whites who did not know the language well, and you find in the vocabularies of Eskimo words copied down by the average traveler an entry stating *nigerk* is a west wind, a south wind, and a north wind. *Nigerk* actually means a wind that blows up the coast. Similarly *kanangnak*, which has many meanings in published vocabularies, has only one meaning to the Eskimos. It is a wind from the sea which may be north, south, east, or west, according to where you are. *Pingangnak* is a wind from the land, from "up there."

To the old-timer, nothing brings home the irony of the phrase "the blessings of civilization" more than the appearance of a dentist in an Eskimo community. Fifty or seventy-five years ago he could not have earned a living in most villages because then every Eskimo had perfect teeth.

One of the marvels reported by early explorers was the way Eskimos could use their mouths as we use a vise or a claw hammer, as an extra tool. The strength of jaw and teeth was startling to us, as for instance their ability to pull a nail from a board with their teeth. In those days every tooth in every Eskimo head was sound. Sometimes the teeth were worn down to the gums with use, and occasionally even broken, but even then they never decayed. Nutritionists and anthropologists believe that where you find decayed teeth you have people who eat carbohydrates. When the white man introduced his food to the Eskimos—flour, sugar, hard bread, and molasses—he introduced tooth decay as well.

Around 1910 it was common in Alaska to meet people who could remember when they first heard of tooth decay and toothache. After shifting from the wholesome primitive diet to a white man's diet, it takes between four and ten years for the first cavities to appear. Village teachers instruct their pupils in tooth brushing and dental hygiene; but few of them mention that before Eskimos learned to brush their teeth they had no cavities, while now they have both toothache and cavities. The teeth of Eskimo villagers are just as bad as ours now; it is not uncommon, alas, to see young Eskimos in their thirties with complete dentures.

Eskimos are quick-witted, as any good ice hunter must be, for a quick death in cold water may be the price of a moment's hesitation. Their above-average intelligence, physical agility and endurance, navigational and hunting skills are combined with a wonderful sense of humor. They also have a remarkable capacity for appreciating, utilizing, and inventing things related to the mechanical arts.

One explorer tells of an Eskimo who possessed a dollar watch, which stopped after two years of use. Its owner proceeded to open the back of it and take it apart, piece by piece.

After carefully cleaning each part he put it back together again so that it worked, although he had never before in his life taken a watch apart. Equally remarkable tales are told of their ingenuity in repairing outboard motor engines they have never seen before.

A completely mistaken but still popular belief is that "all Eskimos live in igloos, and igloos are houses made of ice blocks." The Eskimo word igloo, better spelled iglu, is a general term meaning a temporary or permanent shelter for man or beast. Railway stations, cathedrals, tents, schoolhouses, and family dwellings are all igloos. A snow house is an igloo, too; but its own special name in the Mackenzie dialect is *apudyak*, from *apun*, the name for snow that is lying on the ground, as if ready to be cut into snow blocks for house building. In a few areas white men have told the natives that the word igloo should be reserved for a snow house, and some Eskimos now use it so.

A satisfactory snow house cannot be made of ice. Ice is a good conductor of temperature and would quickly transmit the outside chill indoors. Snow on the other hand is a poor conductor, which means it is an excellent insulator, thanks to the numerous air spaces captured within it. It can be cut in suitable blocks, is light to handle, and easy to shave and carve so that blocks fit neatly and lean at the proper angle. The colder the outdoor temperature, the warmer the inside of a snow house may be safely heated. Experienced travelers who have tried both tents and snow houses in winter camping invariably prefer the snow house as being more comfortable.

The dome-shaped house built of wind-packed snow blocks, and held in place by ingenious engineering and gravity, was confined to an area in central Arctic Canada, east of the Mackenzie River. Use of the snow house extended eastward from there as far as one section of northwestern Greenland, where a small group known as the Polar Eskimos used it. But they were the only Greenlanders who did. South of the Polar

Eskimos, only the earth—and the earth-and-stone—house was used. No Asiatic Eskimos ever used the snow dome structure either.

Alaskan Eskimos never used the snow houses for winter dwellings, as their neighbors to the east did. Some Alaskans knew of the existence of snow houses, a few having learned the skill from explorers or Canadian Eskimos, and then used them as traveling camps. Today all Alaskan Eskimos know about them, and most know how to build a good one. Many have learned through serving in the National Guard, or through reading books like my late husband's *Arctic Manual*, which gives precise instructions and helpful drawings. And, of course, now they have all seen these snow houses in the movies or on television.

Primitive Eskimos in Alaska formerly built their houses of earth. North of the tree line, driftwood was substituted for local spruce to make the frames, and in some places the large bones of whales were used. In spring the Eskimo traditionally left his house to spend the summer in a tent. In the old days the tent was of skins; now it is apt to be of canvas.

One of the Eskimo's remarkable inventions was the way he used gravity in his house to keep the cold out and the warmth in. Winter houses, as made on the north coast of Alaska, had thick earth walls and were always entered from below. The top of the door was always lower than the floor, and usually at the end of an alleyway. You entered the house by going down into a passage and up into the house at the other end. So long as the door was lower than the floor, it never needed to be shut, even at 50° below zero. For cold air is heavier than warm air and cannot rise upwards into a house already filled with warm air. Fresh air was provided by a small ventilator about four inches in diameter in the roof of the house. Cold air could enter from the door below only as warm air was permitted to escape through the ceiling vent. By widening or narrowing this vent, the Eskimo regulated the amount of heated air permitted

This schematic drawing shows how the air-capture principle is used in an Alaskan earth-and-wood house. In summer, the gut window is removed and a ground-level entrance is used. In winter, both window and entrance are closed and the house is entered through a passage by which buoyant warm air cannot escape. This passage is never closed all winter, unless a grid is used to keep out dogs.

to escape and cold air permitted to enter, thus controlling both the temperature and the ventilation of his house. If the house was too warm—and a normal temperature for an Eskimo house might be 80° or 90°—the ventilator was opened wide; if too cool, it would be partially closed. A house with one room, big enough for two average families, needed only three seal oil lamps to keep the temperature at what we would consider more a Turkish bath than a comfortable room temperature. (See above drawing.)

The beach of an old Eskimo village was always its main plaza, the equivalent of our village green. It was the center of activity in both summer and winter. From the beach the hunter went sealing in his graceful kayak, and it was to the beach he returned. If successful, he was surrounded by interested and helpful neighbors. The animal would often be skinned and, if large, divided on the beach. Here, too, families starting off on a journey would pile their children, dogs, and household gear in the family umiak and wave a cheerful farewell as they paddled off. In winter, dog teams and sledges would depart and return via the beach.

Eskimos held views almost the opposite of ours about water and ice. To them ice was something friendly on which they could walk and hunt, which protected them from the treacherous waters below. We usually think of the water as being safe, the ice as treacherous. Eskimos seldom learned to swim. The waters of the Arctic Sea and Bering Sea are too cold, the mosquitoes too many and too hungry.

The Eskimo hunting canoe, the kayak, is no doubt the most seaworthy craft of its size. The spruce driftwood frames are shaped by hand. The pieces, instead of being nailed together, are lashed with wet rawhide, which draws tight as it dries. The sealskin covering fully envelops the boat except for a round deck opening just large enough to receive a man.

In some districts the boat's "manhole" merely fits the hunter's body rather snugly so as to give water little chance to enter; properly, the opening has a raised edge to which the Eskimo lashes the hem of his waterproof coat so that paddler and canoe become one. Water is prevented from entering not merely through the manhole but also through the sleeves and neck of the coat, which are tightly lashed. This hooded raincoat is made from animal intestines, which are dried and sewn together to make a translucent, waterproof garment.

The kayak is about as steady on rough water as a man on a swaying tightrope. Its seaworthiness lies in the skill of the kayaker with his long double paddle, and in the boat and boatmen being a single unit.

Getting in and out of a kayak is a tricky art, accomplished by placing a pike pole or paddle across the boat, with one end

The beach of an old Eskimo village was its main thoroughfare both in summer and in winter.

Eskimo boat frames were formerly shaped from driftwood; now imported lumber is often used.

A kayak overturns easily, but a good kayaker can right it with equal ease.

An expert kayaker must start his training early. The boy's father is usually the teacher—here he demonstrates first lessons in paddling.

resting on ice or on the beach. When a steady balance has been achieved, the kayaker ventures in or out. But don't try it on the basis of these instructions!

When an Eskimo boy is about twelve years old, his father will begin to teach him the difficult technique of handling a kayak, in those areas where they are still used. Long before this time, probably when he was six or seven, he learned to use a gun. He has killed small game and, if lucky, a seal. With his father he has gone on trips by dog team and perhaps made a short sledge journey or two by himself. But a kayak, unless expertly handled, is extremely dangerous. A boy must be serious-minded and industrious to master the art, for a mishap may end in drowning.

Instructions usually begin in a quiet lagoon sheltered from the rough surf. The kayak is so placed on the beach that while afloat on a few inches of water it can still be reached from dry land. The father then gets into the kayak and explains how to hold and manipulate the paddle, demonstrating each step as he tells of it. When this is thoroughly understood, father and son change places, and while the father holds on to the kayak, the boy imitates the motions of paddling. Step by step each maneuver is rehearsed and memorized before the boy takes to the water alone. Even then he is carefully watched and never goes far from shore at first. It takes years of practice to become an expert kayaker but once the skill is acquired, kayak and paddler become practically unsinkable.

Accidents do occur in kayaks, but death usually results not from the kayak overturning once, because a good kayaker can right himself half a dozen times easily, but from the paddler being so fatigued from repeated capsizing that he is unable to right his boat.

While the kayak is a greater marvel of design, nearly the same admiration is due the larger umiak. This Eskimo boat, also skin-covered, is a dory type of craft and, like a dory, extremely seaworthy and capable of long voyages in rough

A skin-covered umiak is light for its size and easily carried. Here Eskimo whalers are carrying theirs to an open lead. All wear goggles to prevent snow blindness.

weather. The average umiak is thirty-five or forty feet long, can transport a two-ton load, yet is light enough for a man and his partner to carry. It is so strong and well fitted for rough handling that the Yankee shore whalers of northwestern Alaska, toward the end of the nineteenth century, exchanged their New Bedford whaleboats for umiaks in pursuing the bowhead whale. An ordinary wooden whaleboat is easily damaged even by small fragments of floating ice, while an umiak going at the same speed will not be harmed at all. A skin boat behaves somewhat like a football when it is struck. A thump is followed by a bouncy rebound. Should a blow be severe, the result might be a cracked rib that can be replaced at leisure, while a hole in the skin is easily patched with needle and thread.

Because it is light, has a flat bottom, and draws only a few inches of water, an umiak can venture safely into shallow places where ordinary boats are unable to navigate.

In summer, to prevent the skin covering of an umiak from decaying, it must be taken out of the water and dried at least every four days—preferably every three. This is easily accomplished. When a party camps for the night, the boat is taken out of the water and tilted on edge. If the weather is fair, the skins will be dry in the morning. Today many umiaks are canvas-covered.

Before the era of jet airplanes and tractor-pulled sledge trains, a dog sled was the only winter means of overland transportation in many parts of Alaska. As long as the ground was snow-covered, which might be for seven months of the year, dog teams were used by trappers, hunters, and mail carriers.

Although still used for sport racing now as well as utility, their numbers decrease each year. Snowmobiles, "ski-doos," and other motor driven vehicles have replaced them.

The so-called purebred Husky dog is a recent development of white dog breeders who carefully mate only dogs of a certain height, color, and fur, deciding beforehand the characteristics desired. These dogs are commonly bred and trained in Maine

The new and the old—a "ski-doo" and an Eskimo sled.

and New Hampshire. They are also used extensively by explorers both in the Arctic and Antarctic.

Some early fur traders sent out by the Hudson's Bay Company to northern Canada were cockney Englishmen who dropped their *h's* and inserted others where they didn't belong. They called Eskimos "Heskimos." An Eskimo dog was a "Heskimo" dog. "Heskimo" was soon shortened to "Hesky," which eventually became "Husky."

Wintertime, when it is a little too dark to do any real hunting, used to be a holiday time for Eskimos. Much of the dark season was spent making sledge journeys to visit back and forth with friends. Eskimo dog teams, once small, became larger in recent times, varying with the wealth of the owner and fashion in a given area. A lead dog is not necessarily the strongest member of a team, but he is usually the most intelligent, for he must interpret the driver's commands. Spirit is the mark of the leader, who may be of either sex and any size.

Thanks to his superior nose, a good leader can often find a trail, made invisible by drifting snow, and guide a lost driver safely home. Lazy dogs are rare, but not unknown. Most sled dogs love to pull and yelp excitedly as they are harnessed for a trip, much as a city dog dances with anticipation when his master appears with a leash that promises an outing.

Helping the dogs cross a difficult place.

Sled dogs are fed once a day and their ration usually is a dried salmon, but they will eat almost anything if they are used to it, seal, caribou, or goose. Dog fights which break out must be stopped immediately, for they may result in the death or maiming of a valuable dog. For this reason dogs are seldom allowed to run loose. After a day's work they are tethered to stakes, out of reach of each other. Good sled dogs are workers rather than pets; for doing their particular job these tough, handsome beasts are unsurpassed.

Eskimo sleds can carry from five hundred to a thousand pounds of load. Formerly, an Eskimo, unless ill, never rode on the sled. He was much more likely to be up front giving the dogs a hand over a rough spot. In extremely cold weather, if a sled is allowed to stop, the runners will freeze fast in the snow. Then it must be rocked loose with a "gee pole," the steering device attached to the right hand sledge runner. White men introduced a kind of rude brake on the back of the sled. It will not stop a runaway team, but is useful for slowing the sled when going downhill.

Some think Eskimos were able to survive in the Arctic because they hardened themselves to it, and so could stand it better than white men. But Eskimos never endured or suffered cold if they could help it; they protected themselves from it in many ingenious ways. They wore truly marvelous, cold-proof clothing which kept them warm however extreme the cold. An Eskimo in his old-style clothing could don a ten-pound caribou skin outfit in January and sit still comfortably outdoors all afternoon while fishing through the ice at 50° below zero.

Sled dogs curl up to sleep in the snow.

Before the white man's influence became strong, Eskimo cold-weather dress consisted of two suits of caribou skin; the inner one was worn with the fur side in, and the other with the fur side out. Each suit was made up of coat, or *attigi*, and breeches which tied about the waist with a drawstring; there are no buttons or buttonholes on truly Eskimo clothing. Both undershirt and outer coat had hoods exposing the cheeks and forehead but protecting the ears. Boots and mittens completed the costume. Inner and outer coats were worn loose, outside the trousers. If the weather became so windy that the garment flapped, a belt was passed around the undercoat to prevent cool air from coming up inside.

It is not enough to own a suit of Eskimo clothing to insure comfortable protection from the cold. It is also necessary to know how to wear it and take care of it. Dry snow and hoarfrost must always be carefully removed before entering a warm house.

When caribou skins have been dried and scraped they are soft and free from odors. Then the highly skilled Eskimo women would fashion them into garments, each of which was a tailor-made work of art. Eskimo seamstresses used to make what is probably the only true waterproof seam in the world. Our bootmakers think a seam cannot be waterproof and usually rub oil or wax into their needle holes. But if an Eskimo sewer saw you rubbing oil on her boot seam she would feel insulted. When a waterboot was finished she would inflate it like a balloon, twist the mouth, and wait for a few minutes to see if any air was escaping. She would hold the seam to her cheek to detect the slightest leak of air, or near a lamp or candle flame to notice the slightest flicker. Caribou sinew was originally used for thread. When a new pair of boots was about

OPPOSITE: A Point Hope Eskimo youth in his coat which has the skin side outside and the fur side inside.

to be worn they would be dampened and the sinew would swell, making the seam tight.

Observing the white people's fashions, Eskimos were quick to adopt first one, then another, item of their clothes. Eventually the miracle of the mail-order catalog reached every village, however remote. Summer dress throughout the Eskimo world then underwent a change. Formerly skin clothing was worn the year round—it was all they had. Now cotton dresses and shirts, rubber boots, blue jeans, and plaid lumber jackets are as popular with them as with us. For summer wear our clothing is more comfortable than theirs; but in winter theirs is far better than ours. Nothing we can offer is nearly as good in extreme cold as an Eskimo caribou skin coat, or an Eskimo-style sealskin waterboot. These two items at least seem destined to survive every onslaught of fashion. An important reason for Eskimos to adopt our clothing is that many now work for wages and have no time to hunt caribou and seals; so there are no skins for making clothing. The fur clothing offered for sale in Alaskan shops is neither good in quality nor inexpensive.

Eskimo mothers used to, and many still do, carry their babies on their backs inside their coats, the child sitting pick-a-back fashion with its little legs around the mother's waist. A belt to prevent it from slipping down was passed under the child in back, brought forward and fastened in front over the mother's breast (see page 65). If the child was young, it was naked and completely hidden from view inside the coat. If older, and the weather mild, it might be lightly clad and its head might protrude from the top of the coat.

Unless his parents are getting all too disagreeably "civilized," an Eskimo child is never punished. The reason is not that Eskimos love their children more than other parents, but rather what they used to believe about the soul.

According to their ancient theory, a child is born with a soul and a body that are equally small and weak. It seemed obvious to an Eskimo that the child would never get along if

Point Barrow seamstresses still make Eskimo skin boots, but their igloos are now heated by natural gas.

it did not have a more experienced and wiser soul to look after it. The first thing a mother did after her child was born was to pronounce a spell and summon the spirit of some person who had recently died.

The Eskimos have no sex indication in their language. They have no pronouns like "he" or "she" in English; they have no sex inflection for adjectives and nouns such as you find in Latin or German. This may be why it made no difference in their thinking whether the spirit summoned was that of a man or woman. In some districts it had to be the spirit of a near relative who had recently died. In another area it might be the spirit of the last person who had died, irrespective of relationship.

It was the Eskimo view of the spirits of the dead that they are strongest just after they first enter the newborn child, and gradually become weaker as the child grows up. Correspondingly, the inborn soul of the child is thought to be weakest at birth and gradually becomes stronger. They believed that when a child is very young its thinking is done for it exclusively by the soul of the dead person, the child's inborn soul having little or no control. If, for instance, a child cried for the scissors it was, in Eskimo opinion, the judgment of the guardian soul that the child ought to have the scissors.

This gave the parents two reasons for yielding. In the first place, it was unthinkable that they were wiser than the guardian spirit. If they refused they would surely offend the guardian, who would thereupon leave the child. With nothing but its own incompetent soul to take care of it, the baby would suffer one misfortune after another. If a man's ears stuck out at the wrong angle or if his nose had a strange shape it was usual to hear people remark that his parents must have punished him when he was young.

According to the old Eskimo way of thinking, during the first few years of a child's life, you were distinctly speaking to the soul of the dead when you addressed the child. Therefore it was customary for those related to the dead to address a baby in terms of that relationship. For instance, if my grandmother's soul had been given to a small boy, I would call him "grandmother" whenever I spoke to him or about him. A mother talking to her baby girl might call her "father," if it was her father's soul which had been given to her daughter. Very confusing to non-Eskimos!

While Eskimos are now Christian and not supposed to believe in guardian spirits, it remains true to this day that Eskimo children are practically never punished physically or forbidden anything.

It is commonly believed that primitive people have simple languages, but linguists tell us the opposite is often true. This is confirmed by the Eskimo language, which (as we said earlier) some believe to be the hardest language in the world to learn.

Eskimo mother and child.

Eskimos do rub noses! But it is an affectionate gesture used between young children and older women.

The active daily vocabulary has more than ten thousand words, most of which are nouns and verbs. Adjective and adverb meanings are supplied by inflection. The inflections are so numerous and complicated that one noun can be written in more than a thousand forms, each with a separate, precise meaning of its own. A verb can have even more forms than a noun!

The structure of Eskimo is so different from English that you must learn a new way of thinking as well as a new vocabulary if you want to speak the language.

For instance, the average American, who wants to learn the language, seeks out an Eskimo who speaks English and, taking care not to be misunderstood, he will hold a knife in his hand and ask, "What is your word for 'knife'?" The Eskimo will answer *"savik."* "And what is your word for 'big'?" is the next question, whereupon the answer, in Colville River dialect, will be *"angirok."* "Now," thinks the white man, "I know how to say 'big knife,' " but as a matter of fact he doesn't know at all, for the Eskimo does not say "big knife" by attaching the adjective for "big" to the word for "knife." Instead he inflects the word for knife by adding a syllable, in this case *pa*, which means big. A big knife is not as we might think *"savik angirok"* or *"angirok savik";* it is *"savipak."* We are accustomed to prefixes and suffixes; the Eskimo also use *in*fixes. That is, they take a word apart and insert a syllable in the middle (rather than at the beginning or end) to alter the meaning.

There are nine cases in Eskimo and they, as in Greek, have singular, dual, and plural forms, giving you theoretically twenty-seven variants of a word, before you add any infixes. (However, it is difficult to make out nine forms in the dual.)

To get an idea of how the inflections work, take the word *iglu* which means a temporary or permanent shelter of any sort. *Iglupak,* means a large house; *iglunguak,* a make-believe or playhouse; *iglorak,* a wooden house; *iglukuk,* a ruined house; *igluliak,* a house that someone built; *iglulik,* that which contains houses, as an island which is inhabited; *iglutun,* like a house; and so on for several hundred variants of one word *iglu.*

The noun is simple compared with the verb. No man has ever worked out the number of possible different ways in which a single Eskimo verb may be used, but an experienced Eskimo linguist has estimated it at a minimum of three thousand.

Under primitive conditions Eskimos always shared their food. No one went hungry while others had plenty; they were well-fed or hungry together. Unlike the Indians, Eskimos had no chiefs, slaves, or aristocrats; in fact, they had no caste. No one held office. No man could order another to do his bidding. Men of judgment and skill were looked up to and consulted because of their superior wisdom or talent, not because of rank. There was equality between men and women; a husband could not *order* his wife to do anything, or vice versa. All common problems of these essentially gentle people were discussed amicably and often at great length. Their often-reported happiness seems to have been the result of good health and of a fortunately natural attitude toward life and death.

Nunivak Island children.

Relatively little of the old ways remain today except their remarkably cheerful spirit and the fine quality of their relations with each other and the outside world. The hunting way of life is fading, but any Eskimo who can, still hunts on the weekend.

The mechanical skills reported by early explorers have enabled the Eskimos to become excellent mechanics, tractor drivers, carpenters, and radio operators. There are Eskimo plane dispatchers, nurses, soldiers, businessmen, artists, writers, hotel- and storekeepers, legislators, newspaper editors, and teachers. For many hundreds of years, existence was so difficult for Eskimos that only the quick-witted, sharp-sighted hunter with good judgment and quick reflexes managed to survive. The present-day Eskimos are his descendants.

In the first century of his contact with the white man, the Arctic Eskimo never stood in awe of western civilization. For in northernmost Eskimo territory the white man was uncomfortable, if not helpless, without Eskimo clothing, Eskimo guides, Eskimo dogs and sledges, and his food had to be shipped in from the outside. The Eskimo was, and felt himself to be, the superior man. Today many Eskimo ideals have been exchanged for those of the white man. Although he is generally quicker, more observant, and more patient than the white man, the Eskimo no longer feels superior.

Among Alaskan natives there is a new surge of pride in all things Indian and Eskimo. This concern for cultural identity is a source of support for peoples who have lost dominance over their lands and a formerly close rapport with families and groups. Reminders of past greatness help them to endure present poverty and the difficulties of living in a white man's world. Now when so few native children speak the languages of their parents there is suddenly a hunger to learn those languages. There is also a rising desire on the part of the parents to preserve and hand on to their children as much of their ancient heritage as possible.

Sadly, up to now, education in Alaska for the natives has always been in English. When Eskimo children would come to school, the teacher, usually someone from the lower forty-eight states with no knowledge of either the Eskimo language or culture, would forbid children "for their own good" to speak the only tongue they knew. They were often punished for doing so! Now for the first time there is a change. In Greenland Eskimos have been taught in Greenlandic and have learned Danish as a second language. In the Soviet Union the Eskimos and other natives have been taught in their native tongues and learned Russian as a second language. But the United States (and Canada, too) remained backward. Now, thanks largely to Michael Krauss, Professor of Linguistics at the University of Alaska, there are thirteen schools where children in Alaska, given a choice between schooling in English and Eskimo, have chosen Eskimo. There will soon be more. In five villages bilingual native teachers are also conducting classes for the first time in the Athapascan Indian language. Studying in a language he knows, a child naturally learns everything much more quickly, including his second language. In the past, by the time an Eskimo finished eighth grade both his Eskimo and English were poor. This was equally true of Indians and Indian languages.

Professor Krauss has been in Alaska since 1960 and has studied almost all the native Alaskan languages. More importantly he is an active promoter and cultivator of Alaskan languages. Rather than embalm a dying language, he prefers, he says, to keep it alive. He turns gifted students into teachers and several have become his assistants. He knows how to involve, interest, and excite natives with bi- or trilingual skills to join his "movement."

It used to be believed that the Eskimo language was one language from East Greenland to Siberia with just a few dialect differences. Recent studies show, however, that the Eskimo language is a *family* of languages, like the Germanic or the Romance languages, with two major divisions called *Yupik* and *Inupiaq.* The Eskimos who live along the Arctic Coast speak the Inupiat dialect. Yupik is spoken by the Eskimos of the lower Kuskokwim and south central Alaska. The St. Lawrence

Eskimos on the back of a small white whale, or beluga.

Eskimo boy with fish-drying racks.

Island and Nome Eskimos speak a dialect of Yupik related to the Siberian Eskimo language. In addition to Eskimo there are two other major groups of languages spoken by Alaskans. They are Aleut, which has both an eastern and western dialect, and is related to Eskimo, and the large Na-Dene group of Indian languages which include the widespread Athapascan-Eyak, Tlingit, and Haida.

The Eskimo language is now taught at the University by Professor Irene Reed. Eskimo and white students work together in the language workshop at the University, translating materials and textbooks into Eskimo to be used in teaching the lower grades. Fifth grade children who have been taught in Eskimo will be ready to study most subjects in English and will have a better command of English than their predecessors did. Formerly when an Eskimo child went to school he was separated if not alienated from his parents by language. In the case of older students who had to leave their villages in order to get a high school education the alienation was usually permanent. They would return without the native skills they needed to live comfortably in a native-oriented village—hunting for the boys, skin sewing for the girls, etc.—and with no use for the white man's knowledge they had learned so laboriously. Their education was seldom good enough to permit them to compete successfully with the non-natives in the cities.

Professor Krauss plans a center at the University where the native people themselves will become the leading students and cultivators of their own languages. They will look to their parents for the fine points of language and custom, and will be drawn closer by what they learn and the resulting exchange.

CHAPTER IV

Fact
and Fable

ALASKA IS A LAND OF EXTREMES—of the very old and
the very new, of ancient Eskimo and Indian cultures
and modern pulp mills and rocket ranges. Here you
will find, side by side, glaciers and strawberries, dog teams
(although they are dwindling in number) and airplanes. A skin
boat, the design of which has not changed for a thousand years,
is fitted with the latest model outboard motor.

The state of Alaska contains a confusing variety of climates
and terrains. Between rainy southeastern Alaska and the
northernmost treeless Arctic slope are magnificent snow-clad
mountains, vast forests, broad prairies. Alaska has the third
largest river in North America, the meandering Yukon, placed
by its length and drainage basin after the Mississippi and
Canada's Mackenzie. It has innumerable small lakes, no large
ones.

One of the commonest mistakes made about Alaska is that
it is a frigid country, so chilled that there are no summers. But
two thirds of Alaska lies below the Arctic Circle, and even at
Point Barrow, its north tip, the lowest winter temperature is
slightly above the lowest records of North Dakota, Wyoming,
and Montana. In central Alaska the maximum heat of summer
is about equal to that of New York City. The U.S. Weather
Bureau has recorded temperatures of 100° F. in the shade at

Fort Yukon, just north of the Arctic Circle, 99° at Fairbanks, just south of the Circle, and similar highs for other places. The heat in the Arctic is usually humid. In summer the days grow longer and longer until, for a short period in northerly latitudes, they are twenty-four hours long, and the sun never sets. The heat is continuous; there is no cooling-off period as in the tropics. While the summer season is much shorter in the Arctic than in the tropics, without the relief of cool nights it seems harder to endure.

We *expect* Alaska to be cold and are not disappointed. The winter of 1971 was a bitter one and on January 23 all Alaskan and U.S. records for extreme cold were broken when a temperature of −80° F. was recorded at Prospect Creek, a site in the foothills of the Brooks Range on the proposed Prudhoe Bay–Valdez pipeline.

Unless you have been in the north in summertime, it is hard to visualize and impossible to describe the terrific number of mosquitoes that exist. Formerly, no European traveler dared move into the bush country, or out upon the prairies, without a headnet, gloves, and heavy clothing lashed tightly at wrist and ankle to protect him against the pests. Thanks to the invention during World War II of several effective mosquito repellents, one can now wear light clothing without being at the mercy of biting insects.

Mosquitoes do not breed as well in a lake as in a swamp; they prefer many small puddles of water. In most of the Yukon Valley, when you dig below the surface a few inches, the ground is permanently frozen. Last winter's snow water and yesterday's rain cannot penetrate downward through the hard-as-concrete frost but stays on the surface to form innumerable swamps, each an ideal breeding place for mosquitoes.

OPPOSITE: Close-up views of different kinds of glaciers are seen on a tourist trip to the Juneau Ice Fields.

In summertime Juneauites may swim in surroundings of incomparable beauty.

Eternally frozen subsoil, or permafrost, as it is now called, underlies the northern two thirds of Alaska. Experts tell us it occurs beneath one fifth of the entire earth's land surface. Half of Canada and much of the northern Soviet Union have permafrost. Wherever it occurs, lack of underground drainage results in thousands or, more likely, millions of lakes, ranging in size from small puddles to many square miles. When you fly over permafrost country it has a typical look—half or even more of the ground below is covered by lakes of all sizes and shapes. These provide landing places for pontoon planes in summer and wheel- or ski-equipped aircraft in winter.

It is no accident that Alaskans fly more than any other people in the world. The distances between cities are often great, the highways are few, and the terrain is various, rugged, and difficult. Often an airplane is the only means of reaching what would otherwise be an isolated place. In 1971 Alaska had a certified pilot for every forty residents and one in eighty-two Alaskans owned his own plane. The state carries more passengers and flies more cargo tonnage per year than any other state.

Small pontoon planes are a common sight in Alaska.

The Great Circle polar routes to the Orient can save as many as four thousand miles on flights between Europe and Asia by flying directly. Anchorage and Fairbanks have become international airports for the more than six aviation companies now offering flights to Asia via the forty-ninth state.

Along the suburban lake shores of Anchorage you will see rows of neatly moored pontoon planes awaiting their owner-pilots. Most are small craft which take off or land on any of Alaska's numberless lakes. Families living in Alaska's largest city use them to "get away from the congestion of city life." Planes bring spare parts, machinery, mail, fresh food, and relief workmen to remote mining and oil developments. They pick up and deliver trappers, fishermen, scientists, tourists, or week end campers. They taxi doctors, nurses, and patients in and out

Dramatic mountain scenes unfold on the flight to Anchorage from the south.

of the bush and permit a minister to visit the farthest borders of his parish. Nowadays prospecting for metals and oil is done from the air; so is mapping, in a fraction of the time formerly required. Children go to school by plane in Alaska, salesmen visit their customers, and some prosperous women at Point Barrow are said to fly south regularly to Fairbanks, a thousand-mile round trip, to shop and have their hair done.

In tiny, distant villages, the bush pilot still plays an important role. Usually one man does all the flying to and from a small village. He knows the terrain by heart and has made friends with the local weather. He will fly in weather other flyers would not dare attempt. He is a combination mailman, ambulance driver, personal shopper, and Santa Claus. Sometimes he is the only link between the village and the outside world. Of necessity he is their confidant; he is their newsbearer, and usually is adored by the villagers. If he has any unusual personality traits they are discussed with relish and woven into a kind of folklore that follows him for the rest of his life.

There are two railroads in all of Alaska: the Alaska Railroad, whose main line operates from Seward to Fairbanks, and the White Pass and Yukon, which runs through only twenty miles of Alaska on its way from Skagway to Whitehorse, in Canada's Yukon Territory. The Alaska Railroad is government-operated and has 537 miles of track. In summertime the daylight trip from Fairbanks to Anchorage is a favorite with tourists, for it cuts through the heart of Alaska, with magnificent scenery all the way.

One of the most popular stops on the Alaska Railroad is at Mount McKinley National Park, where the chief attraction is the mighty mountain the Indians call *Denali,* meaning "home of the sun." Mount McKinley is one of the most dramatic sights in a land which abounds in stunning scenery. The light tan granite mass, crown of the Alaska Range, climbs upward to a height of almost four miles! No other mountain in the world rises so far above its own base. The upper two thirds of the peak is permanently snow-covered, and often takes on a pinkish glow at sunrise and sunset.

McKinley Park is the farthest north and second largest U.S. national park. It was created by an act of Congress in February, 1917, and covers over three thousand square miles. Its snow-capped peaks and grinding glaciers slope down into spruce-forested valleys. The park abounds in wildlife. Caribou, giant Alaska moose, handsome white Dall mountain sheep, grizzly bear, wolf, wolverine, and lynx are some of the animals which might be seen by a lucky tourist from a train window as the railroad speeds through the park.

When the Alaska Road Commission was formed in 1905, there were less than a dozen miles of passable wagon road in Alaska. Today the famous Alaska Highway connects Canada with Alaska. This road, almost sixteen hundred miles long, was completed during a wartime emergency in November, 1942, thanks to the almost superhuman efforts of both Canadian and American military and civilian construction men. As soon as it was finished, in a record-breaking eight months, military equipment began streaming in from the States through Canadian Edmonton and Whitehorse, to Fairbanks, the Alaskan terminus. After the war, tourists followed, in growing numbers each year.

In 1948, spurred by a tense world political situation, the U.S. military examined Alaska again. Her geographical position gave her new value in an atomic and hydrogen bomb age. Facing the Arctic Sea on the north, almost touching Siberia on the west, and bounding the North Pacific to the south, Alaska stood virtually undefended. Huge costly military installations were built along with new and improved roads with which to service them.

OPPOSITE: Horseshoe Lake in Mount McKinley National Park is typical of the grandeur and beauty of the state.

The highway system of 1970 includes a 3,215-mile network of all-weather paved roads. They connect the ice-free ports of Valdez, Seward, and Haines with interior Alaska's principal cities and military installations, as well as with the lower forty-eight states. A secondary system of 3,635 miles connects farming and industrial areas to the main network.

A new string to the Alaskan transportation bow is the recently inaugurated Alaska Marine Highway System. It consists of a ferry fleet ranging in size from the Swedish-built *M. V. Wickersham*, which carries 1,300 passengers, to the *Chilkat*, which accommodates only 59. Its purpose is to provide transportation for the Alaskans who live in the coastal and island areas of the state with the equivalent of a land highway system. The beautiful, protected waterways of the Alexander Archipelago offer a natural communication and travel route both for Alaskans and the growing number of tourists. In southeastern Alaska the ferries connect Ketchikan, Sitka, Wrangell, Petersburg, Juneau, Haines, Skagway, Prince Rupert and Vancouver in British Columbia, and Seattle, Washington. In the western system Cordova, Valdez, Homer, Seldovia, Kodiak, Seward, and Anchorage are served. In addition to passengers the ferries carry autos, trucks, cargo vans, and other land vehicles. The ferries are extremely popular in summer but operate at a loss in winter.

In recent years, as the speed and range of airplanes increased, so did our understanding of Great Circle air routes. The Arctic or Polar Sea, surrounded by the world's most powerful nations, acquired a new and to some, ominous, importance. The old east-west air routes are as dated as biplanes. The new routes lead north or cross the Arctic regions slantingly. If hostile planes ever approach our land, we believe they will come not from the Atlantic or Pacific but from beyond the North Pole.

In response to this new orientation the Distant Early Warning Line of radar stations was created in 1952. Known more familiarly as the DEW Line, the function of its numer-

Stern-wheelers were once a familiar sight on the Yukon River.

ous outposts, ringing northern Canada and Alaska, is to warn of the approach of enemy planes. Building the DEW Line resulted in the largest invasion of the Arctic in terms of men, ships, materials, and equipment in the history of the Northland. Every known means of transportation was utilized, and a few new ones invented. By ship, by plane, by long tractor-driven sledge trains, by river barge, and by giant new rubber-wheeled vehicles that could travel over snowy roadless tundra in summer and winter—all converged in the course of a single year on North America's northernmost continental shore. Hampered by the need for developing special methods to deal with short summers, ice-choked waterways, permafrost, muskeg (a thick, spongy waterlogged carpet of mosses and sedges), cold temperatures, and humid summer heat, the engineers pushed on. The successful completion of the DEW Line in a surprisingly short time was a victory over stupendous obstacles.

A hazard associated with life in the far north is the uncertainty of radio reception. Radios have a way of suddenly, without warning, going dead. Sometimes, too, noisy atmospheric static will blot out the signal. Since such interruptions might be disastrous in wartime, the Defense Department, as part of the general fortification of Alaska, built a huge communications network designed to keep us in touch with the farthest Alaskan outposts, whatever the weather. The code name of the

project, while secret, was White Alice, and it still bears the name.

On November 30, 1956, the first link of White Alice's chain of stations was finished. Each of the forty-seven stations was equipped to receive and transmit signals, using a method of radio relay never before used on such a large scale. Good telephone and telegraphic communications are maintained between stations, whether skies are stormy or clear. Huge scoop-shaped, sixty-foot-high antennas, each weighing 100 tons, are used to beam signals into the troposphere, the five-mile layer

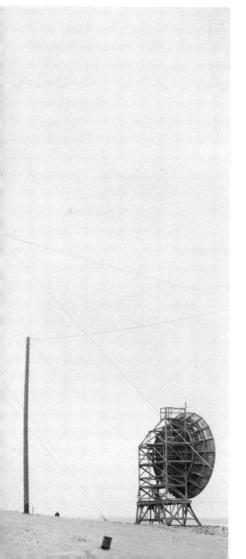

The once curious pattern of buildings and equipment forming a DEW Line station is now commonplace in the north.

of air that extends upward from the earth. In the troposphere the signals are "scattered," and only a tiny fraction of the energy sent out arrives at the receiving antenna. Here it is amplified until intelligible. Identical antennas, spaced at distances of up to two hundred miles, receive the signals and re-transmit them if necessary.

White Alice was designed primarily to enable the Air Force to keep in touch with radar outposts, but all government departments, civilian telephone and telegraph agencies, as well as the people of Alaska, benefit in peacetime from the system.

For centuries Alaska's principal interior highways were rivers. In summer they served as liquid avenues for Eskimo kayak and umiak and Indian canoe. Later the white man introduced paddle-wheeled, wood-burning steamboats and other craft. After fall freeze-up, rivers are transformed into broad ice highways on which formerly dog teams, horse teams, and more

This White Alice station in the Matanuska Valley has twin 60-foot antennas and a horn antenna atop a 175-foot tower.

For centuries Alaska's rivers were her only highways.

recently motor and tracked vehicles would travel. More freighting is being done throughout the north by caterpillar tractors, or "cats" as they are called, pulling long trains of heavily loaded freight sledges. In building the DEW Line, a new kind of vehicle was introduced. This was a huge houselike truck, with giant rubber-tired wheels, taller than a man, which rolled effortlessly across the roadless, snow-covered frozen muskeg. Teams of drivers ate and slept in them, taking turns driving. Snow cats and skidoos are now common, but hovercraft and Rolligons, vehicles with huge air-filled rollers, are the vehicles of the future.

Any heavy-wheeled vichicle that drives across the roadless tundra kills the fragile vegetation in its tracks. When the vegetation dies the sun's rays begin to thaw the exposed earth, melting the permafrost below. When the permafrost melts the landscape is disfigured and permanently scarred.

A vehicle which may offer one solution to the protection of the environment problem is a curious looking "truck without wheels, a tractor without tracks," called a Rolligon. Instead of wheels or tracks the Rolligon has wide, big, thin-walled, ultra-low pressure air bags. It can operate in roadless areas without tearing up the vegetation cover as tractors or heavy trucks do. It travels easily in summer across swamps, sand, waterlogged muskeg and tundra; and in winter thru snow and even along frozen river beds without danger, since the weight it carries, more than ten tons, is evenly divided on its huge eight rolling air bags. These roller bags replace wheels and lightly press the vegetation cover instead of cutting into and

The extraordinary-looking Rolligon travels anywhere in all seasons and every kind of weather and doesn't damage the fragile Arctic vegetation.

The hovercraft offers one more solution to Alaska's transportation problems.

wounding it permanently as other vehicles do. The thirty-five-foot-long Rolligon travels easily across rough country, steep hills, the soft rubber bags conforming to whatever unevenness is encountered. Rolligons have demonstrated that they can travel in midwinter without snowplow assistance and that they can perform ordinary construction work without harming the environment.

Another vehicle that seems hopeful for safe Arctic use is the hovercraft, which operates on a cushion of air either on land or water.

Every tiny village in Alaska, even a lone wilderness camp, has a shortwave radio receiving and sending set. The two-way radio is vital for survival in many parts of Alaska, especially the sparsely settled areas. It combines the virtues of newspaper, telephone, telegraph, and a visit across the back fence with a neighbor. It is the link with civilization, the source of help in troubled times, the bearer of tidings, good and bad. If a plane is overdue, you first hear of it on the radio. If a listener has news of it, he reports. If hours go by without word, rescue plans take form and are put into action.

Sometimes homey messages are heard through the innumerable privately owned two-way radios. Recipes and gossip are exchanged. Chess games are played, a move or two a day, by players hundreds of miles apart. Strangers in the area are sure to be mentioned, their business and personalities discussed, and, usually unbeknownst to them, their movements will be followed with friendly interest.

The shortwave radio dispenses medical information to isolated villages, especially in emergencies, where a plane would be unlikely to arrive in time, or when weather prevents the flight. Operations have been performed by schoolteachers and others with little or no knowledge of surgery, step by step, according to instructions from a doctor who may be a thousand miles away and who calmly, quietly asks questions and gives directions. Countless babies have been delivered by this unusual hospital of the air waves.

A better, far more sophisticated method of dispensing medical information is scheduled for 1972, when the world's first regional satellite communications network begins operations. Twenty-six Alaskan towns and villages, many of them remote, will be able to get quick, accurate diagnostic and treatment information from staff members of the big city hospitals. The connecting link which makes it possible is NASA Satellite ATS-1. A federal grant from the National Center for Biomedical Communications provided the necessary financing.

Weather reports, by which the aviator lives, are broadcast on shortwave radio at regular intervals and by request. Nowhere in the world, I believe, is there so much talk of weather as in Alaska. Good weather means flights on time, mail, groceries, machinery, and people delivered on schedule. Bad weather means waiting and more waiting, no mail, no flights, boredom, frustration, standstill. Where the plane is one's only link with "outside," talk about cold fronts, cloud ceilings, fog, moon, and visibility is pertinent talk.

In 1969 oil and gas surpassed fisheries as Alaska's second largest industry. The federal government ranks first! Alaska nevertheless leads all other states in the value of its fish products, $191 million in 1968. Salmon is still the most valuable fish, especially since the roe, formerly discarded, is now utilized. King crab production, which rose spectacularly, has declined; some think it was overfished. Scallop production began on a large scale in 1968, Tanner crab increased in 1969, and shrimp production blossomed in 1970. There is a large foreign fishery in Alaskan waters, largely Russian, Japanese, and Korean, which takes more fish than the Alaskans themselves do.

In the 1950s the most important industry was "defense."

Petersburg's harbor is crowded with fishing boats.

More than $100 million was spent in 1956 alone building airfields, bases, radar and communications lines. This created employment for thousands of Alaskans and brought outside specialists to the land. In 1969 the Department of Defense and related agencies and the Atomic Energy Commission spent more than half of the total federal budget of about $750 million in the state. Military personnel in Alaska outnumber the total of workers in farming, fishing, forestry, mining (including oil and gas construction), and manufacturing combined. Few outsiders understand how much Alaska remains a kind of "colony" of the military establishment and other federal government agencies. Three quarters of all Alaskan employment and income comes directly or indirectly from government spending, according to Dr. Arlon Tussing. Dr. George W. Rogers, another University of Alaska professor and Alaska's most respected economist, titled one of his papers "Alaska— the Federally Owned State." Federal spending has helped keep up Alaska's notoriously high prices and living costs.

The forestry industry was almost nonexistent in Alaska until the fifties but by 1969 it produced $110 million worth of products. Wood in different forms accounted for 80 percent of all exports to Japan, and the industry is expected to grow. The Ketchikan pulp mill has been operating since 1954, one in Sitka was completed in 1960, and a third big mill in Juneau begins operations in 1973. The Tongass National Forest is the source for the Ketchikan and Sitka lumber operations, and tree harvesting is done according to good forestry and conservation principles. The state of Alaska also owns important forestry lands north and west of Haines, near Cape Yakataga, and on the southern part of the Kenai Peninsula. Ironically, most of the lumber used in Alaska comes from the Pacific Northwest states, and most of the lumber produced in Alaska goes to Japan. Ninety-four percent of the lumber produced in 1968 was exported.

A fast-increasing boost to Alaska's economy is the tourist

The famous Juneau Ice Fields are a dazzling sight on a sunny day.

trade. Each year in greater numbers, travelers flock to the state by car along the Alaska Highway, by leisurely boat through the Inside Passage, but most of all by air. Thanks to excellent connections, a Texan or a New Yorker, with a two-week vacation, can travel north of the Arctic Circle, view the midnight sun, photograph totem poles or the tallest mountain in North America, or set foot on a startlingly beautiful glacier in southern Alaska. He can visit Indian and Eskimo villages, talk with their inhabitants, and watch them perform ancient dances.

For that indispensable ritual, part of every holiday to a far place, he can purchase innumerable fascinating native handicrafts to take home for souvenirs.

Gold mining, once a mainstay of Alaska's foremost industry, has declined steadily since the forties when gold prices were fixed. Crude petroleum leads all mineral products with natural gas, often found in conjunction with oil, coming third. Second place goes to sand and gravel production, which rose spectacularly during the 1964 earthquake reconstruction and remains important for highway and airport construction. Coal is still mined but production has decreased since 1967.

The Chilkat Indian dancers from Port Chilkoot are part of the current revival of native arts and crafts.

Farming is an industry in the fertile Matanuska and Tanana valleys, but there is stiff competition from foodstuffs flown in from outside. Except for the steady Pribilof Island yield, fur production and fur farming have, like gold, faded to ghosts of their former importance.

The colorful whaling industry used to be important in Alaska and was revived after the Civil War. The two chief uses for whalebone then were to stiffen women's corsets and to make buggy whips. Tailors used it also to make men's shoulders appear broader and squarer than they actually were.

In summer whaling ships used to sail through Bering Strait and east along the north coast of Alaska. The first vessels wintered in 1889 at Herschel Island, just west of the Mackenzie River delta, in what was supposed to be U.S. territory but was later determined to be Canadian. Many whales were captured north of Bering Sea and the Alaskan mainland.

Ships used to winter two or three times on a voyage. The crew usually numbered forty-nine because law required any ship carrying fifty or more men to have a doctor aboard, and the owners were eager to avoid this expense. The largest whales gave two thousand pounds of bone, which, at four dollars per pound, netted eight thousand dollars. The record catch on a single voyage was sixty-nine whales, the average whale giving perhaps one thousand pounds of bone. The profits were impressive for some—but not for the men before the mast. They worked for a percentage, sometimes as low as 1/200th share of the profit, and easily managed to spend their earnings on what the skipper sold them from the slop chest. These percentages were called "lays." Those of the crew members were very small; the captain's very large, sometimes enabling him eventually to buy his own ship; and the lion's share went to the owners.

This romantic and, for the owner, lucrative business came to a sudden close around 1906. That year more than a dozen ships had wintered at Herschel Island, or points east; thereafter no more than two or three ships wintered, and these devoted themselves almost wholly to trading.

The failure of the whalebone industry was caused by three things which happened simultaneously. Women stopped wearing heavily-boned corsets, men stopped using buggy whips because the automobile was coming in, and somebody invented a substitute called "featherbone." Whalebone dropped in price from four or five dollars per pound to fifteen or twenty cents and, indeed, was difficult to sell at any price except in very small quantities.

Eskimos still hunt whales for food at Point Hope. Here they have harpooned one.

While commercial whaling died out in Alaska, Eskimo whaling continued, as it had for centuries before the white men took it up. Commercial whalers usually had taken only the whalebone, or black baleen, wastefully discarding the rest of the huge mammals. But to the Eskimo, whale meat is food, and even one or two whales caught per season might spell the difference for an entire village between a year of plenty and a year of want. They love its nourishing meat and consider the skin, with an inch-thick layer of blubber attached, a special delicacy. It is called *maktak,* or *muktuk,* and it is eaten raw.

In the areas of Point Hope, Wainwright, and Point Barrow, the Eskimo umiaks are still brought out in the early spring each year for repairs, and a period of great excitement and entertainment for the villagers is begun. Boats are fitted, gear is readied, and the umiaks take to the open waters. Luck and the weather will decide whether many or no whales will be taken. The outcome is of vital concern to the villagers. But just as important as food is the appeal of whaling itself as the hunters confront its dangers, accept its challenges, and display, both individually and in groups, their remarkable seamanship and skill.

CHAPTER V

Capitals
Old and New

W HO WAS RESPONSIBLE for our purchase of Alaska? Most historians credit William Henry Seward, our secretary of state under Lincoln. Seward reasoned that in order to properly defend the United States we needed Alaska to dominate the North Pacific, and Greenland and Iceland to dominate the North Atlantic. He advocated that we buy Greenland and Iceland from Denmark, and Alaska from Russia; but he succeeded only with the Russian part of his plan. Negotiations were opened with Russia for the purchase of Alaska, a price of $7.2 million agreed upon, and at 4:00 A.M., March 30, 1867, the Treaty of Purchase was signed by Secretary Seward, acting for us, and by Baron de Stoeckl, acting for Russia.

At the time of the Purchase the capital of Russian America, as it was called then, was Sitka. To this day it remains the most Russian city in the state. Everywhere in Sitka there are reminders that it was once a thriving imperial metropolis, with a gay social life; indeed, it was a cultural center for the entire northwest coast. This city, which all Sitkans, and many non-Sitkans, consider the most picturesque in Alaska, was founded in 1799 when a Siberian trader, Alexander Baranof, moved there from Kodiak Island, site of the first Russian settlement. He arrived with thirty Russians, several hundred Aleuts, and

The old Russian capital is considered the most picturesque city in the state, especially by its loyal inhabitants.

a charter from the Russian America Company, which gave him exclusive rights to all profits that might be derived from any resource whatsoever in the Russian colony. Baranof was under orders to stop the trade in furs and ivory being carried on by other nations. He was also to protect the Indians' lives and property, to feed them in time of disaster, to educate their children, and if possible, save their souls.

The Indians, unaware of this intended kindness, resisted the newcomers vigorously. Ten of the thirty Russians had constantly to stand on guard. The local people would capture and kill any single man or small group of Russians. In 1802, when Baranof was away visiting Kodiak Island, the Indians captured the post, killing all the men and taking the women and children prisoners. Baranof returned in 1804 and rebuilt the village, naming it New Archangel. The Tlingit Indian word, Sitka, which means the "best place," had long been in use, however, and the new name did not stick. Hostility between the Indians and the whites continued until as late as 1855, when a battle showed a score in dead and wounded of twenty-one Russians and sixty Indians.

At the end of the eighteenth century, when San Francisco was still a mission, Sitka became the largest settlement on the entire Pacific Coast, a center of trade and civilization. Into the exquisite Bay of Sitka, peppered with tiny spruce-covered islets and dominated by towering Mount Edgecumbe, came clipper ships from New England stopping off on their way to China, English trading ships, ships from Kronstadt on the Baltic, Spanish ships, French ships. Here Yankee traders matched wits with Tlingit Indians, the Yankees frequently getting the worst of the bargain. It was the gayest, most brilliant city of a huge wilderness empire.

On October 18, 1867, Sitka witnessed the dramatic formal ceremonies which transferred possession of Alaska from Russia to the United States. Russian soldiers in dark red-trimmed uniforms and U. S. troops in full dress stood at attention in front of the governor's castle, making a brave show despite the rain. The Commissioner of the Imperial Ruler of all the Russias said the necessary words and the U. S. Commissioner received the land for its new owners. The Russian flag was lowered and the American flag raised in its place, to the accompaniment of tears from the Russian ladies and salutes from the batteries and ships' guns in the harbor. Later most of the Russian families returned to Russia; only a few remained, and their descendants still live in Sitka.

Reminders of Sitka's Russian past turn up at Easter time, when decorated eggs are traded, and *kulich,* a sweet holiday bread, is eaten. Two Christmases are celebrated, one at the usual time, the other according to the Russian calendar. Another reason for the continuation of some old Russian customs is that Sitka remains the spiritual center of the Russian Orthodox Church in Alaska.

Saint Michael's Cathedral, which housed many rare icons and souvenirs of old Russian America, was destroyed by fire in 1966. The basement, however, remains and here services are now held. Fortunately, the artistic and historical treasures were saved from the fire.

Today Sitka is a modern town of almost four thousand, famous for its beauty and pleasantly mild climate. Except for the airways, you approach it from the sea through a beautiful narrow channel that runs between the shore and Japonski Island. Here you see for the first time the peak of Mount Edgecumbe, an extinct volcano often compared to Fujiyama. The innumerable little green islands that surround the old capital offer calm lagoons for sailing or sheltered landing places for pontoon planes.

The famous Sheldon Jackson school and college, founded in 1878 and the oldest Alaskan school in continuous operation,

Mt. Edgecumbe outlines the horizon at Sitka.

Sheldon Jackson College was founded in 1878.

is at Sitka. Its splendid museum contains interesting Eskimo
and Indian exhibits collected by Sheldon Jackson early enough
to include many rare and unique specimens. The mask collection is particularly wonderful and rich.

Sitka has hotels, a fine government hospital, a library, cold
storage plant, and the famous Pioneers Home for aged sourdoughs, or old-timers, built on the old Russian parade ground.
A pulp mill financed with Japanese capital employs about four
hundred people full time. It brought some ten Japanese families to Sitka, which turned out to be interesting for both Sitkans and the newcomers.

The Mount Edgecumbe Boarding School, formerly run by
the Bureau of Indian Affairs, is in the process of becoming a
state school.

Sitka National Monument Park has a splendid collection
of totem poles. Eighteen in number, they were gathered from
many parts of Alaska for an exhibit in the 1904 Saint Louis
Exposition. When the fair was over, Alaska's Governor John

Totems guard the entrance to Sitka National Monument Park.

Brady succeeded in having them returned to Alaska and placed in Indian River Park, which is now a national park.

After the Purchase, Sitka remained the capital of Alaska until 1900, when the rapidly growing city of Juneau was named as the new seat of government. Governor Brady and the executive offices remained in Sitka until 1906; thereafter the new governor took up his duties in Juneau.

Juneau is still the capital. It stands on Gastineau Channel at the water's edge, framed by the steep, timbered slopes of Mount Juneau and Mount Roberts, which tower above the city. There is so little space between the mountains' edge and the water that one wonders how a town came to be built on this particular spot. The answer is easily found—gold. Juneau's history, like that of other places in the state, begins with the discovery of the yellow metal. Two prospectors, Harris and Juneau, found gold at Silver Bow Basin in 1880, and before the next spring arrived, more than a hundred men were camped at the site. This was the first gold rush on Alaskan soil. Harris and Juneau disagreed for two years about naming their camp and finally a town meeting of miners was held so that a decision might be reached. A compromise was effected by calling the town Juneau and the district Harrisburg.

From the time of the U. S. purchase until 1897 there was a black period of lawlessness in Alaska's history. With no civil law or administration for maintaining order, murder, burglary, and drunkenness were the order of the day. The gold stampeders in the late 1890s and 1900s, although without civil authority, created their own form of local self-government, on the order of New England town meetings. Together with such sporadic administration as was possible through the army, navy, and custom service, this served until 1912, when the Alaskan legislature was created.

Gold mining continued to be the chief industry in Juneau

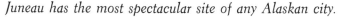

Juneau has the most spectacular site of any Alaskan city.

Juneau's links with the rest of Alaska and the world are by air and water.

for more than half a century, until, in the 1940s when the price of gold was fixed by the federal government and mining costs rose steadily, it no longer paid. The huge Alaska Juneau Mine, once the largest gold mining operation in the world, reckoning by tonnage, stands silent and empty today. It once employed almost a thousand men and had an annual payroll of more than a million dollars. Today fishing and lumber are more important. A $100 million pulp mill will be completed by 1973.

Juneau's connections with other cities in Alaska are by water and air, except for Douglas. Douglas is her twin city; it stands on a wooded island across a narrow channel spanned by a bridge and since 1971 has been part of the borough of Juneau.

This is a modern town of thirteen thousand people, with tall buildings set on steep hills, reminding one of San Francisco in feeling if not in size. Administrative offices of the federal government are housed in a new many-storied building, and there is a fascinating, handsome, modern Alaskan state museum. Juneau has one of the seven community colleges that are part of the University of Alaska complex. It is a ferry stop on the Alaska Marine Highway System. The favorite gathering place for legislators, visitors, and townfolk is still the coffee shop of the Baranof Hotel, where issues are hotly debated and many social and business matters settled.

There is a splendid harbor at Juneau, crowded in season by salmon and halibut fishing vessels, which has excellent docking facilities. The capital has a modern airport, with a connecting

The old Russian Orthodox church in Juneau.

automobile road running through another of Alaska's startling landscapes. Here are spectacular mountains, brilliant glaciers glistening in the sun, set against dark green, tree-covered slopes, all contributing to a colorful scene of splendor. Nearby Mendenhall Glacier, one of the few in the world accessible by road, is a seventeen-mile-long ice stream that provides an important tourist attraction, but is also enjoyed and thoroughly explored by native Juneauites. On a sunny day its crevasses reflect the strong blues of sky and surrounding water. Picnicking within sight of it is a local tradition. In Auk Lake outside Juneau you may swim comfortably within sight of a white glacier!

Auk Lake with Mendenhall Glacier in the background.

Interesting Islands

Looking into Tomorrow

U P NORTH where the Bering and Arctic seas meet and
Siberia and Alaska seem to be reaching out to join
hands are two rocky little islands, the Diomedes.
Standing on Little Diomede you can see across to another
hemisphere, into another day of the week! Little Diomede is
part of Alaska in the Western Hemisphere, while Big Diomede
belongs to the Soviet Union in the Eastern Hemisphere. Only
a narrow strait separates the islands, but through this strait runs
the International Date Line, on the other side of which is a
new day. When it is Monday in Alaska on Little Diomede, it
is Tuesday in Siberia on Big Diomede. You can look into
tomorrow from Little Diomede or, if you are standing on the
larger island, you can peer into yesterday.

The Eskimos who lived on the islands were once related
and, with little thought of date lines and international boundaries, used to visit back and forth by boat in summer, or afoot
in winter when the strait was frozen over. This was a privilege
reserved for Eskimos only, and during World War II this
informal and friendly interchange ended. After the war, in
1948, when eighteen Little Diomeders thought it time to
resume the old ways, they went across to the bigger island to

visit and trade as they had often done in prewar times. They were arrested by Soviet officers, imprisoned, but eventually released. Now it doesn't matter whether you are Eskimo or not, it is inadvisable to set foot on Big Diomede. Rumors persist, however, that in midwinter Eskimos from both islands sometimes meet and visit in the middle of the frozen strait.

Vitus Bering was a Dane who began his long service in the Russian Imperial Navy at the age of twenty-three. Peter the Great placed him at the head of an expedition charged with determining whether or not the continents of Asia and America were connected. In 1725 he embarked on what has been called one of the most remarkable undertakings in the history of exploration and science—really a series of expeditions, lasting many years and involving hundreds of men. On August 16, 1728, Saint Diomede's day, he sighted two islands and named them after the saint. A heavy curtain of fog prevented Bering from seeing what he had traveled so far to discover, the coast of America, and he turned back soon afterward. What a trick of fate this was! Had the weather been good he would have returned to Saint Petersburg triumphant. Instead, his first three years of intense labor were considered wasted and the opening expedition of the series counted a failure.

It is a common belief that once there was a land bridge between Alaska and Siberia by which the animals of North America and Asia migrated back and forth. The Diomedes, placed where the distance between the two continents is smallest, only fifty-six miles, were probably part of this bridge. Some believe that twenty, thirty, or forty thousand years ago, when man first arrived in America from Asia, he was able to walk across Bering Strait on an ice bridge that was part of the glacial age. Others think a land bridge existed then. More likely the first human discoverers of America came in skin boats similar to the Eskimo umiak, which we know is capable of long sea voyages and of carrying sixty or more people. Neither of the Diomedes has a harbor, but that would not have mattered, for skin boats of that day would have been as easy to haul up on a rocky shore as the boats the islanders use today.

The design of an umiak is considered an ancient one and is thought to have changed very little. The eight umiaks still in use on Little Diomede today have the same sleek lines of their ancestors, but ribs instead of being made of driftwood, laboriously spliced, are now made of imported hardwood and steam bent. Now too, likely as not, there is an outboard motor attached to the stern.

This village with its cobbled streets on Little Diomede is within sight of Asia.

Seal oil may still be used for heating and cooking on Little Diomede Island, but it is burned in an enamel pan instead of a soapstone lamp as formerly, and the wick is made of canvas instead of pussy willow fuzz or moss. Where hunting large game animals is still the chief means of support, fur clothing will be found too, for it is lighter, more comfortable, and more effective against the cold than white man's dress. But the furs are supplemented by cotton dresses worn indoors by the women and cotton parkas worn over the furs to keep them dry.

A common sight throughout Eskimo villages in Alaska now is a mixture of the two types of clothing.

Both of the treeless Diomedes rise from beachless shores, with almost perpendicular sides. On the smaller island the houses of Ignaluk, the only settlement, are perched in terraces along the steep sides of the island. In 1970, eighty-two people lived in the village, which at first glance resembles a medieval town. It has streets paved with cobblestones, complete with gutters draining the water. Unlike most primitive Alaskan Eskimo earth dwellings, the Diomede houses are in the main built of rocks held together with clay. Bits of driftwood are utliized whenever they can be found, supplemented in recent years by imported timber. Roofs were formerly of walrus skin, but shingled roofs are not uncommon now.

The deep surrounding waters supply walrus, still the mainstay of the Diomede diet, but also whale and seal. A few bears and foxes are taken too, but all are supplemented by store-bought canned milk, tea, sugar, flour, and cigarettes. Old sea ice, which freshens with age, is the only water supply.

All the able-bodied men in the fifteen families at Ignaluk are members of the Eskimo Scouts of the Alaskan National Guard. There are only seven of them now, and the population of the granite, flat-topped island is dwindling. In summertime the families, driven like so many other Eskimos by a need for money to purchase gasoline, sugar, flour, and outboard motors, cross in their skin-covered umiaks to the mainland to earn what they can. The Diomede Islanders, with their wealth of walrus-tusk ivory, have become excellent carvers, and their cribbage boards and figurines bring the highest prices in Anchorage and Nome. But the life struggle is harder now that it was before the coming of the white man. The Diomede Islanders retained their old ways longer than less isolated villagers on the mainland. They were the lucky exception to the typical rule. Now, with their dependence on white men's goods and their need to earn cash money, they are, alas, typical.

Group of fur seals, Pribilof Islands.

Misty Home of the Fur Seals

Two hundred and fourteen miles north of the nearest land are five islands that make up the Pribilof group, also known as the Seal Islands. They are Saint Paul, Saint George, and three much smaller uninhabited islands, Otter, Walrus, and Sealion Rock. The seals arriving here each year are probably the only aquatic animals in the world that have the honor of being escorted to their summer home by the U. S. Coast Guard, which protects them from being illegally hunted at sea.

The islands are named after their Russian discoverer, Gavriil Pribilof. In 1786, while sailing among the Aleutians, he noticed the migrating seals and decided to try and follow them to their breeding grounds, the location of which had long been a tantalizing mystery. He sailed northward and by chance took an almost direct route to the rookeries. He landed on June 12 and named the new island Saint George, after his ship. So foggy is this area that it was a year before Saint Paul, the larger island, was sighted, although it is only forty miles away.

Since then the misty Pribilofs have become famous as the largest fur seal rookery and the greatest single source of furs in the world. The precipitous islands are volcanic in origin and for nine days out of ten in summer are enveloped in fog. Here there are only two seasons, foggy wet summer and dry windy winter. The damp summer climate and the numerous sheltered rocky areas are so perfectly suited, however, to the needs of the breeding fur seal that 80 percent of the world's fur seal population come here to have their young. The Pribilof seal differs from fur seals living in the Southern Hemisphere and is unlike the much more widely distributed, smaller, hair seal. The latter animal has a short, stiff-haired pelt, in contrast to the fur seal's silky, luxurious coat, and is hunted for food and fuel by Eskimos from Siberia all the way to Greenland.

Neither of the two larger Pribilofs has a harbor, and navigation is dangerous. The group lies near the southern limit of scattered ice in Bering Sea and detached pieces of arctic pack may be seen bobbing offshore between February and May. The steep coasts also provide excellent seasonal housing for a hundred species of bird life including auklets, cormorants, gulls, murres, kittiwakes, and sea parrots.

Once Pribilof discovered the breeding grounds of the fur seal, wholesale slaughter followed. It has been estimated that between 1799 and 1834 two million animals were killed. From 1835 until the Alaska Purchase, it was forbidden to kill female seals, with a hope of perserving the diminishing herds.

Later, when the route of the annual migration was discovered, came pelagic sealing, the taking of seals at sea. Schooners would follow the herds from the Oregon coast to the Seal Islands, killing as they sailed. They would lie off the islands waiting for the mothers as they went to sea to secure food for their young. This was double murder. If a mother didn't return her baby died of starvation, since a seal will nurse no pup but her own. In an effort to stop this wanton slaughter the United States called conferences and passed laws, but to no avail. The laws drove the sealers to register under foreign flags, and they managed to get many seals despite revenue cutters patrolling the sea.

By 1910 it was estimated that indiscriminate hunting had reduced the fur seal population from three million to one hundred and twenty-five thousand. In that year our government took charge of the rookeries and finally negotiated a treaty with Great Britain, Japan, and Russia, by which pelagic sealing was outlawed. Since then, through care and scientific management, the herd has increased and in 1971 numbered 1.2 million. Each year a small percentage of young males between three and four years of age are killed for their pelts. The skins are sold at fur auction and then made up into the handsome long-wearing coats that are once more fashionable. The 1971 harvest, which took place between the June 24 and the last day of July, was thirty-two thousand. In recent years the average has been between forty and fifty thousand, fluctuation depending on the number of available young males. For a time in the late fifties, because of too great an increase in the herd, some females were taken, but that practice has been discontinued. The value of the skins in 1971 was more than $2 million.

In 1940 Japan denounced the fur seal treaty and proclaimed that her sealers would take animals wherever and whenever they could. In 1957 after the war, an interim North Pacific treaty was agreed to by Canada, Japan, the Soviet Union, and the United States. It gives Canada and Japan a percentage of the seal skins taken commercially by the United States and the Soviet Union. It has been renewed twice, the last time in 1966.

Names given to members of a fur seal family are curious.

The mature male is called a "bull," his wife a "cow," and their youngsters are "pups." A bull and his wives constitute a "harem" and a congregation of harems is a "rookery." The three-year-old males are called "bachelors" and they are the ones that are killed each year.

Fur seals are first cousins to the sea lion. They live from twelve to fifteen years, and the male usually weighs four to six times as much as the female. After she is three years old the cow gives birth to one pup annually, soon after her arrival on the island. When the pup is weaned, mother goes to sea in search of food for her offspring and may travel great distances, remaining away for days. On her return, by a secret process known only to mother seals, she can always spot her own child among the thousands of pups waiting on the beach.

Although the Pribilofs are treeless, they are covered in summertime with deep green and yellow green vegetation, brightened with the color of flowering plants. There are Aleut villages on Saint Paul and Saint George. It was from these settlements, as well as from the Aleutian Islands, that puzzled and dismayed natives were evacuated to Admiralty Island during World War II. They have since returned and today number about seven hundred. Most of them are engaged in the fur seal industry, under the supervision of the Bureau of Commercial Fisheries, Department of Commerce.

Musk-Ox and Reindeer

In clear weather Nunivak Island, the second largest in Bering Sea, is visible in all directions for about thirty miles. Because it is surrounded by shoals which make boat approaches extremely dangerous, explorers and traders alike gave it a wide berth for many years. This permitted Nunivak's Eskimos to retain their ancient ways longer than their mainland cousins. As late as 1926 Nunivak Islanders still wore bead and walrus ivory labrets, or lip ornaments, discarded long before by other western Eskimos. They still adhered religiously to elaborate ceremonies relating to seal hunting and social life in general. Then as now, walrus, seal, and fish were plentiful round the island and the Nunivakers were prosperous.

Although the shift from old to new ways came late to the island, which lies off Alaska's western shore about midway between the Aleutians and Seward Peninsula, it was nevertheless inevitable. With the intrusion of a new culture came the missionary, the schoolteacher, and eventually the bush pilot and his plane-load of parcels from mail-order houses. To the Nunivak Eskimos, the change brought not only a new way of life but also two new animals for their island.

In 1935 and 1936, thirty-one musk-ox, originally imported from Greenland, were moved from the mainland to Nunivak, which is a national wildlife refuge. The herd has now grown to almost six hundred. With danger of overgrazing the island imminent, about a hundred and fifty were transported to various parts of the Alaskan mainland by the Alaska Department

Musk-ox mother and calf at the University of Alaska's musk-ox farm.

of Fish and Game. These strange, prehistoric-looking beasts formerly roamed throughout the northern part of North America as far south as Kentucky. In mainland Alaska, probably the last native musk-ox was killed south of Point Barrow around the 1870s. The tough, sturdy animals are perfectly adapted to Arctic life, and defend themselves easily against all northern predatory animals except the grizzly bear. Bears were the reason for moving them to Nunivak, where there are neither bears nor wolves. Musk-ox do not fear wolves, for wolves will not attack them unless they come upon a lone old animal or a lost calf.

Contrary to their reputation, musk-ox are seldom aggressors. When alarmed they usually run to the top of the nearest knoll, making a defensive formation with big animals on the outside and calves in the center. They charge singly, usually, each one making a short powerful rush of from ten to fifteen yards, then whirling, running back to the herd, facing about and backing into line. Several polar expeditions have reported musk-ox calves that domesticated themselves and became camp pets.

Close to the skin of a musk-ox is a downy wool of incredible softness called *qiviut* by the Eskimos. The short curly hairs of this underfur are interspersed with longer, stiff hairs, similar in texture to a horse's mane, called overhair or, more often, guard hair. The qiviut is shed every spring, but the guard hairs which protect it remain permanently. Short-legged and thick-bodied as they are, during the shedding season in April or May their legs are often invisible. The shedding wool drags in long tags after the animals, and wisps may be picked up from the ground and bushes. The Eskimos call the musk-ox *umingmak*, the bearded one.

In 1954 John Teal transferred seven musk-ox calves from the Canadian Arctic to his Vermont farm to start the Institute of Northern Agricultural Research, now known popularly as the Musk-Ox Project. A decade later he captured nine males and twenty-four female calves on Nunivak Island and took them to a farm at the University of Alaska where they have now increased to over a hundred.

Domestication of the musk-ox was undertaken to provide a source of cash and employment for Arctic people who didn't want to leave their villages. To pay for food, fuel, and shelter that they can no longer obtain for themselves, many natives must leave their family for a part of each year to earn money. Rather than raise musk-ox for their meat, the far more valuable qiviut is the preferred end product, for it is worth fifty dollars a pound. An animal produces between five and a half to seven pounds of wool annually and therefore can earn over four thousand dollars during its twenty- to twenty-five year lifetime.

Qiviut is half the weight of cashmere, lighter, finer, longer-fibered, and softer. It is extremely warm and will not shrink even when washed in hot water. The sale of qiviut products has been a great success despite the high prices; scarves begin at fifty dollars.

Musk-ox cows carry their young for about eight months and babies weigh about twenty pounds at birth. They are easily tamed and taught to drink milk from a can fitted with a nipple. At six months they are dehorned, which protects them from one another and prevents injury to the herders.

In 1968 a project specialist visited Nunivak Island to conduct the first training class for Eskimo women in knitting with qiviut, which has an attractive pale brown color. Patterns are based on traditional Eskimo motifs and a new graphic method of stitch notation was invented for knitters speaking little or no English. Women in more than ten Alaskan villages are now busy, some of them earning up to fifteen hundred dollars annually in their spare time, a most welcome supplement to meager Eskimo incomes.

The next project step will be the establishment of a musk-ox farm in one of the Alaskan coastal villages. Breeding stations have already been established at Old Fort Chimo in Quebec and at Bardyu in Norway and are planned for the Northwest Territories, Greenland, and Iceland also.

Nunivak's other introduced animal is the reindeer, our name for a wild caribou when it is domesticated. Originally imported from Siberia into Alaska during the nineteenth century to supplement the native's dwindling supply of food, the dark brown—sometimes spotted—animals increased rapidly until at their peak they numbered half a million. Through neglect and ignorance they were almost wiped out during the late forties. In a few cases reindeer were placed on islands that had no wolves, their chief enemy, and permitted to run freely. They increased in number sufficiently to tax the grazing facilities of the islands, posing a threat of overgrazing and eventual starvation. Reindeer "moss," properly a lichen, is their main food. It is an extremely slow-growing plant, requiring many years to renew itself.

The Nunivak reindeer herd numbers about ten thousand now and all are descendants of ninety-nine animals landed on the island in 1920. The Bureau of Indian Affairs erected a reindeer slaughtering plant to take care of the natural increase, for if protected from wolves a herd will double in three years. Until 1965 about two thousand animals a year were slaughtered and the meat used to supplement native diets locally and elsewhere in Alaska. Several years later ownership of the herd was turned over to the Nunivak natives. Attempts are now being made to replace the old slaughtering plant and to obtain federal meat inspection facilities on the remote island so that reindeer meat may be shipped to the lower forty-eight states where federal inspection is required. A Nunivak Island Reindeer Committee consisting of Eskimos, government representatives, and an experienced businessman has been appointed to look after the herd during this transition period.

Reindeer are permitted to wander freely throughout the island all year. At butchering time they are herded and suitable animals picked for slaughtering. Reindeer are sensitive and if startled tend to stampede, milling round and round in clock-wise, tight-packed formation. All dogs in the neighborhood are tethered and kept out of sight at this time, for they resemble wolves sufficiently to frighten the reindeer and might start them running.

Eskimo women skin the animals. Flesh and fat are scraped from the skins, which are then hung up outdoors to be dried by wind and sun.

Despite the fashionable invasion of white man's food, thinking, and technology, there are some areas where Eskimo craft is still preserved because it surpasses anything the white

Baling reindeer skins on Nunivak.

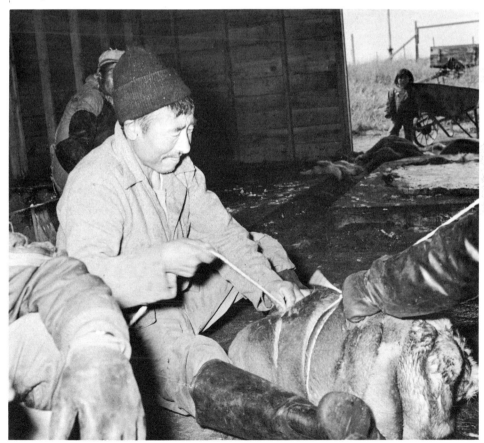

Ugrug *or bearded seal mask from Mekoryuk.*

man can devise. The skin boat is a good example. Wooden boats are in use on the island, to be sure, but for gliding swiftly and silently through ice-choked waters in search of seal or other game, the light, slender kayak is still supreme. Umiaks, too, still compete successfully with wooden boats on Nunivak, because they are lighter and have a greater carrying capacity for their size. As mentioned before, they require extra care—the skin cover must be dried out between voyages to prevent rotting— but then they never require scraping and painting as wooden boats do.

At Mekoryuk, the main settlement on Nunivak, the population has dwindled to 249 in 1970. The island is famous for its beautiful ceremonial masks depicting bird or animal images, which may be seen decorating the walls of Alaska homes as well as museums throughout the world. The masks are still made and sold to visitors or to the Native Arts and Crafts Service which distributes them to gift shops throughout Alaska.

Shrimp Capital of the World

Kodiak, site of the first Russian colony in Alaska, is in the Gulf of Alaska on northeastern Kodiak Island. Damaged in the 1964 earthquake, it was rebuilt and soon became the largest fishing port in dollar volume in the United States and the largest shrimp port in the world. Almost ten thousand people live in Kodiak. Like Sitka, it has many reminders of its Russian past. Russian names are encountered everywhere. The first Russian Orthodox church was built here and is still functioning. Father

Blue onion-shaped domes top the still-active Russian Orthodox Church on Kodiak Island.

Herman, who led the first Christian mission to Alaska in 1794, was canonized and became Saint Herman in March, 1969, in impressive ceremonies.

The present-day Historical Society and Museum is in a building constructed by Alexander Baranof's men. Since 1966 Frank Brink's "Cry of the Wild Ram," a pageant depicting the early history of Russian Kodiak, is given annually in a beautiful outdoor theatre. The entire town is involved in the production, which is a great tourist attraction.

The harbor is crammed with fishing vessels, and many processing plants handle and freeze the shrimp, crab, halibut,

Kodiak's Historical Society and Museum are housed in a building dating from the first Russian settlement in Alaska.

Many souvenirs of the Russian-American period of Alaska's history, including icons, furniture, and household goods brought to the New World by Russian settlers, are preserved in Kodiak's museum.

and scallops caught in neighboring waters. The navy still maintains a station built in 1940 on Kodiak and it is a stop on the Alaska Marine Highway.

Islands of the Smoky Sea

The treeless Aleutian Islands are the tops of a partially submerged mountain range which once linked Asia and America. Forming a continuation of the Alaska Range, they curve westward in a great arc to separate Bering Sea on the north from the Pacific Ocean to the south. From Alaska Peninsula to the outermost end of the chain almost eighty volcanoes have been counted, more than half of which have been active in historic times.

A surprising number of people think of these islands as Arctic, but actually they lie between eight hundred and one thousand miles south of the Arctic Circle, in the latitude of England and northern France. In addition to innumerable islets and rocks, they consist of fourteen large and about fifty-five small, mountainous islands. The five main groups are the Fox Islands, closest to the mainland, the Islands of the Four Mountains, the Andreanofs, the Rat Islands, and the Near Islands, named for their nearness to Kamchatka but farthest from the rest of Alaska.

The Aleutians are among the foggiest places in the world. When cold air meets warm air, the mingling produces fog. At the Aleutian Islands the icy waters of Bering Sea sideswipe the warm Japan current of the north Pacific Ocean. Result—what aviators call "pea soup" fog.

There are said to be only two seasons here, a rainy, foggy, cool summer and a comparatively mild, somewhat clearer winter. The thermometer never drops as low as zero, but cold, wet winds of high velocity blow across from Siberia to combine with warm air masses from the south. They produce rain, fog, mist, and snow. Good weather is rare and brief, shifting swiftly as the winds change. "Uncertain" is a word often used to describe Aleutian weather; "terrible" is probably the adjective *most* used.

"Williwaw" ("woolie" to the Yankee whalers of old) is a term familiar to all Aleutian Islanders but known too along other Alaskan coasts. It is a violent puff of wind that sweeps down suddenly with great force from a mountain slope. Because they come without warning and successive gusts change direction unexpectedly, williwaws are dangerous to vessels at sea or in harbor. A boat will toss wildly and is likely to break out her anchor or capsize. A man cannot stand against a strong williwaw, and sailors, particularly those on small sailboats, have a healthy terror of them.

Williwaws, fog, and sudden storms have been responsible

for some of the nicknames applied to the Aleutians. Birthplace of the Winds, Islands of the Smoky Sea, and Cradle of the Storms are among the more romantic ones. During World War II many soldiers stationed there invented new ones, few of them romantic and most of them not even polite. A rueful joke that made the rounds was "if the Japanese capture the Aleutians, it will serve them right." The men who had to fly bombing and scouting missions from Aleutian bases had cause for fear and complaint—fog, as well as Japanese gunfire, took so many of their young lives.

The innumerable passes between islands have strong and treacherous tidal currents. Contrary to popular belief, these channels are ice-free throughout the year. Sea ice never forms in the Aleutians except on the inner bays. The ocean is equally free of ice north and south of the chain. If you spent ten years atop the highest of the Aleutians with a telescope looking north into Bering Sea you would never see a cake of ice. It is only when you travel eastward toward Bristol Bay that floes begin to appear in the north.

The mild, highly intelligent Aleuts who inhabit these islands are of the same racial stock as the Eskimos. Although their languages were once the same long ago, when the people separated their languages changed in different ways. Now although related in structure and vocabulary, they differ enough so the people cannot understand one another. The Aleut language is dying; only an estimated six hundred Aleuts are able to speak it today. Like the Eskimo, the Aleut is of medium size, with short legs, large head and face, Mongoloid eyes, straight black hair, and a scanty beard. They probably came to the islands from the mainland of Alaska in two separate migration waves. We think the first was more than four thousand years ago, the second within the last thousand years. It is thought that in their heyday they may have numbered twenty thousand —a far larger number than any neighboring Alaskan areas could support. But the riches of the surrounding sea were plentiful in sea lions, seals, and whales. Salmon and fowl were available too and, of great importance, ample supplies of driftwood for boat, tool, and weapon building. Aleut culture successfully aimed at developing self-sufficient individuals in a cooperative community. Few genuine Aleuts survive today—estimates vary from one tenth to one sixteenth of their original number. Over half of them live outside of the Aleutian Islands now, chiefly in the Pribilofs and on the Soviet Komandorski Islands. Census lists always show a higher figure because they include all native peoples living in the Aleutian area. To further confuse the picture, some Eskimos call themselves Aleuts and some Aleuts call themselves Eskimos. The 1970 census listed 6,851 Aleuts.

The Aleut decline began soon after the Russians found the islands in 1741. Traders followed the explorers and were greeted hospitably by the friendly Aleuts. It is one of the darkest stories of European relations with "natives" that the Russians returned kindnesses with cruelties, thefts, and brutal killings, virtually enslaving the entire population. Aleuts were forced to spend their time hunting the fabulous sea otter and, of course, to turn over the skins to the local representative of the Russian America Company. Both the Aleut and the sea otter decreased rapidly thereafter. Umnak Island, which once sheltered twenty-two villages and two thousand people, had by 1970 a single village, Nikolski, with a total of only fifty-seven inhabitants.

The sea otter, one of the most precious of all furs, played an important role in early Alaskan history. Single skins have brought $1,500 in the memory of men still living. Four times heavier than the land otter, the sea otter is about four feet long and may weigh anywhere from thirty to ninety pounds. They were practically exterminated during the eighteenth and nineteenth centuries by Russian fur hunters, or *promyshlenniki.*

It all started when the members of Vitus Bering's last

expedition, sick and dying of scurvy, were shipwrecked on Bering Island. Here they found sea otters in abundance. The fresh meat cured their disease and gave them strength to build from the wreckage of their vessel a tiny namesake, the *Saint Peter*. Its limited cargo space was filled with fresh meat for the voyage back to Siberia, and into the remaining spaces the crew stuffed as many otter skins as they could. When they arrived in Petropavlovsk in 1742 they found the skins fetched enormous prices. In the Chinese market otter skins were the costliest, valued even above sable. This inspired Siberian hunters to extend their hunting operations across Bering Strait to Alaskan waters.

So successful and greedy were the hunters that by the turn of this century the sea otter was thought to be extinct. Around 1910 the U.S. government forbade the taking or sale of these animals, imposing heavy fines for the mere possession of a skin. Slowly a tiny remnant of the once huge herd began to increase.

In 1939 on Amchitka Island, largest of the Rat Island group, an interesting experiment in animal conservation began. As the "pods," or colonies, of sea otters grew, surplus animals were transplanted to other suitable islands to further increase their number. Today there are more than forty thousand sea otters in Alaska waters and more than a thousand off the California coast. They are now so numerous that five to seven hundred are permitted to be taken by hunters each year lest they increase beyond the capacity of the local food supply. Otters are one of the few tool-using animals. The beguiling mammals use a stone to crack the shells of the crab, mussel, abalone, and other shellfish they eat.

While the Russian role in the Aleutians was generally a grisly one, an exception to the rule can be found in the life of Father Ivan Veniaminov. He was not the first Russian missionary of Greek Orthodox faith in the Aleutians, but he was the first to master the difficult Aleut language and to interest himself in Aleut culture and welfare. In a native skin kayak, he paddled from island to island questioning people about their traditions and customs. For a decade following 1824 he lived in Unalaska, preaching and teaching, but also learning. Adapting the old Russian Cyrillic alphabet for the purpose, he created an Aleut alphabet which greatly aided the people in preserving their wonderfully complicated ancient language. Veniaminov opened a school for Aleut children. He translated the Catechism and the Gospel of Saint Matthew into Aleut and wrote an Aleut grammar. His painstaking writings are still source material for anthropologists and linguists. Under the name of Innocent, Father Veniaminov finally achieved the highest office of his church when he became Metropolitan of Moscow.

Many Russian traders settled in the Aleutians, marrying native girls. Modern Aleuts have a large measure of Russian blood; almost all have Russian names. Their church remains the Russian Catholic, or Greek Orthodox, church.

A thrill of horror swept Alaska and the United States when, six months after Pearl Harbor, in June, 1942, the battleground of World War II shifted from far places to North America itself. The Japanese bombed Atka and Dutch Harbor. The following day they occupied Attu, the outermost Aleutian Island, killed the schoolteacher who was trying to send out news of the invasion, and took his wife and every other resident of the island prisoner. They were taken to Japan and interned in prisoner-of-war camps, where many of them died. Kiska Island was occupied, too.

Shortly afterward everyone living in the Aleutians was evacuated to the mainland. Forced to leave behind all they owned, the Aleuts were taken to evacuation camps in southeastern

OPPOSITE: An Aleut housewife blowing air through washed seal intestine. It will be stretched, dried, and eventually made into a waterproof coat.

An Aleut wedding in the Russian Orthodox Church. The crowns, symbolizing holiness of marriage, must not rest on the couple's heads.

Alaska where many of them, for the first time in their lives, saw trees. The only battle of the war on U.S. soil occurred in May, 1943, when American infantry, after nineteen days of shelling and sniping, recovered Attu from the Japanese.

At the war's end in 1945, Aleuts were permitted to return to their homes—all, that is, except the Attuans. Attu, one of the Near Islands, fourteen hundred miles west of Anchorage, is a lonely, isolated spot. Its buildings had all been demolished in the war. Although the Attuans were eager to go home, the government decided their island should not be reoccupied and that Attuans should live on Atka Island, closer to the mainland and easier to defend. So now Atka, some five hundred miles east of Attu, about midway in the chain, has the honor of being the most westerly community in North America—much more westerly than the Hawaiian Islands. The island is rugged and volcanic, and smoke still issues occasionally from its northern end. There is a Russian Orthodox church and also a government schoolhouse at the settlement, which numbered eighty-eight in the 1970 census.

In summertime, most able-bodied men on Atka leave the village for the Pribilof Islands where they work in the fur seal rookeries. Their summer earnings are the sole cash income in the village; without it they would have great difficulty getting through the winter.

Sailing westward from Alaska Peninsula you would pass Unimak Island, the first of the Aleutian chain, separated from the mainland by narrow Isanotski Strait, or False Pass. This is the largest of the eastern Aleutians, and the home of magnificent Shishaldin Volcano, locally referred to as Smoking Moses. Several times in recent years Shishaldin, which rises majestically for almost ten thousand feet, has been in eruption. Faint wreaths of smoke and vapor still drift from its summit, making a striking picture, for the volcano is largely snow-clad. Pogromni Volcano, whose Russian name means "desolation," is a smaller conical peak near the western end of the island, also snow-covered.

Akutan Island, largest of the Krenitzin group, was once an important whaling station. Commercial whaling is no longer a local industry, but the Aleut settlement remains.

Unalaska, the next large island, is mountainous, and during the greater part of the year its higher elevations remain snowy. Makushin Volcano, more than six thousand feet high, forms the peak of the island. Unalaska Bay, on the northern shore and open to Bering Sea, is one of the most important bays in western Alaska. It contains the harbors of Iliuliuk Bay, Unalaska Harbor, and Dutch Harbor.

The port of Unalaska, founded by Solovief in the eighteenth century as a fur trading station, was officially opened as a U.S. customs port during the Klondike gold rush. It had been much used by American and Russian vessels for years before that since it is a good halfway station for ships plying between Seattle and Nome.

Dutch Harbor in Unalaska Bay was once a flourishing

Unalaska is the largest town in the Aleutians. Note the Russian Orthodox Church to which the Aleuts still belong.

settlement and the capital of the fur sealing industry. The U.S. Navy built a base here which in June, 1942, was the scene of the first Japanese attack upon North America.

Atka Island, the largest of the Andreanof group, contains Korovin Volcano, which rises about four thousand feet. Aleut women on Atka, and on Attu also, were famous for their exquisite baskets of beach grass which often took two or more years to complete. Wild rye, which commonly grows on Aleutian beaches to a height of four to five feet, was the grass used

for making mats as well as baskets. It was gathered in the fall as it began to turn brown, split into thin strands, and bleached. Then the long process of weaving began, with the grass stored in something damp to keep it moist and pliable. In more recent times, bits of colored embroidery silk were woven with the grass to produce beautiful designs. The result was a watertight masterpiece, prized by Aleut and white man alike. Most of these old baskets are to be found only in museums or in the collections of a lucky few, but the art is being revived again as part of the renewed interest in native arts and crafts.

The rest of the Andreanof Islands are relatively unimportant, but they have strange, musical names like Koniuji, Igitkin, Kanaga, Tanaga, Kavalga, Unalga, Ulak, and Ilak.

Kiska, one of the Rat Islands, has more level ground than most of the islands and the best harbor in the area. In World War II it was occupied for a time by the Japanese after the attack on Dutch Harbor.

At the end of the chain are the Near Islands, Agattu, and the outermost Attu. Across the International Date Line, the Komandorski Islands, belonging to the Soviet Union, form a continuation of the Aleutian arc, reaching toward Kamchatka and another way of life.

Other
Alaskan Cities

ANCHORAGE IS THE LARGEST, richest, most powerful
city in Alaska. Surrounded by the magnificent snow-
clad Chugach Mountains, it is the big business center
of the state. Oil and aviation companies have their main head-
quarters here as does the Alaska Railroad, and the city's port
is the busiest in Alaska. New office, hotel, and home building
goes on constantly but never seems to catch up with the city's
needs. Anchorage, with its surrounding suburbs and villages, is
big enough to have luxurious skyscraper hotels, shopping centers, chain and department stores, and thus, unlike most other
Alaskan cities, competition, which brings down the high cost
of living a little. Anchorage has radio and TV stations, two
competing daily newspapers, and the great advantage of easy
access to savage wilderness country for the hunting, shooting,
fishing types and nature lovers who want to get away from the
daily city grind.

Alaska's first international airport in Anchorage played a
pioneer role in the beginning of Europe-to-Asia Great Circle
air routes. In November, 1956, Scandinavian Airlines inaugurated the first line to fly directly across the geographic North
Pole on its Copenhagen-to-Tokyo run. Now six different companies offer shortcuts via Alaska, and one company sells round-
the-world flights from Anchorage via Siberia and Russia. The

High-rise buildings now interrupt the view of snow-capped mountain peaks in Anchorage.

largest, most luxurious planes in the world land here now, bringing many Europeans and Asians, especially Japanese, to Anchorage. The latter are a familiar sight in many Alaskan cities, not only as tourists, but as directors and employees of the numberous Japanese-financed enterprises that now exist in Alaska.

Eskimos visiting or working in Anchorage are often difficult to distinguish from the Japanese, which isn't surprising since their physical beginnings thousands of years ago were linked. An experimental Arts and Crafts Center has been established recently in Anchorage to provide help for all native artisans whether Eskimo, Indian, or Aleut. Training, research opportunities, and expertise in marketing and small business development is being offered. Anchorage also has a handsome

Historical and Fine Arts Museum, one of the city's major tourist attractions. In addition to its general exhibits it sponsors an annual Alaska Festival of Native Arts, doing its part to encourage and raise the artistic level of the native culture and craft revival that is taking place throughout Alaska.

With the growth in population and wealth a movement began in Anchorage to have the capital of the state shifted there from Juneau. The Juneauites were indignant, and by rallying the extremely competitive cities of Fairbanks, Ketchikan, and Nome and acting together, the attempt was defeated.

An indication of the resiliancy of Anchorage and its fifty thousand inhabitants is its recovery from the 1964 earthquake. Worst in Alaskan and North American history, it was the second most severe recorded in the world. In a terrible five minutes $200 million worth of damage was sustained as great

Parking meters and a building boom are part of the scene of Alaska's largest city.

gaps opened in the earth. With government aid and its own dynamic spirit, within two years most of the damage was repaired and the city was flourishing once more.

An event of importance to all Alaska occurred just outside Anchorage in the late summer of 1957. An oil strike was made by the Richfield Company close to the city, which started an "oil rush" throughout the Kenai Peninsula. Up to that date every drop of fuel oil burned in Alaska had to be imported, and costly freight charges added to the retail price. Excitement swept the country and crowded other news off the front pages of all newspapers when word of "oil in our back yard" first reached Anchorage. True, the navy some years before had drilled for oil and found it around Umiat and elsewhere in the Point Barrow region, but that had been in a naval reserve area and held no meaning for the average citizen interested in keeping down the cost of his fuel bills. The rest is history.

Anchorage is the home of the largest native hospital in Alaska, as well as the Arctic Health Research Center, both vital factors in the war against tuberculosis and other diseases.

In 1940 the first detachment of U.S. troops arrived in Anchorage to start work on a new air base. Today the huge installations of Fort Richardson and Elmendorf Field have swelled both the temporary and permanent populations, and increased the prosperity of local businessmen, and increased inflation too. Anchorage is only one spot, but a central, key one, in a tremendous network of airfield bases, DEW Line, and White Alice stations which the military establishment still maintains.

Long distance and even intrastate communications constitute one more of Alaska's problems. The systems now in use combine many small local companies, plus White Alice and other military systems. Until January, 1971, when they were sold to R.C.A., the army was in charge of all Alaskan long distance communications. Much of the equipment dates from World War II and has been expanded to its maximum capacity. With a growing population, a rough climate, and absence of roads, satellite communication offers a solution to the problem. Satellites have been in use successfully on a small scale since 1970. Comsat has offered the state a multi-purpose plan which is under consideration that would use the sample Talkeetna station to serve the Anchorage area for long distance and TV communications. It would expand to serve Fairbanks as well and, with the construction of other ground stations, the entire state.

The Golden Heart of Alaska

The word *gold* has a glamorous sound! It has power, too, enough to lure thousands of hopefuls to Alaska around the turn of this century, and it meant different things to different people. Some who came wanted a fortune, overnight if possible. Some were fleeing the crowded, dirty cities and wanted only untainted air to breathe and lots of space. Many were running from trouble, real or imagined—family, work, or money trouble. For some older men it was the last, lone hope of making a "success." A few women, considered very daring, came too. Idealists, cynics, workers, loafers, adventurers, and writers— they all poured into the territory. There was plenty of room for them in Alaska.

Some lucky few struck gold, but far more eventually gave up prospecting and turned to keeping shops, restaurants, and roadhouses. The fortunate ones who knew a trade like carpentering, found it more lucrative in the long run than panning gold. These "sourdoughs" formed the nucleus of many Alaskan towns, including Fairbanks.

In 1902 Felix Pedro discovered gold on what is now Pedro Creek. By September of the same year enough prospectors had arrived to hold a meeting, appoint a recorder, and name the place "Fairbanks" after their vice-president.

News of the strike spread rapidly, but it was followed by disappointment when the gold-bearing bedrock was found to be buried eighty to a hundred feet under muck and gravel, much of it frozen hard in the permafrost. This meant that expensive equipment was needed to extract the gold. It was hard on the lone prospector, but it prevented the kind of mushroom development that nearly or quite wrecked several other gold rush towns.

In many sections around Fairbanks the rich pay dirt was worked out long ago. In the 1950s the most productive gold mining operation in Alaska was that of the U.S. Smelting, Mining and Refining Company outside Fairbanks. Mass production mining undertaken by million-dollar corporations took over the major portion of the industry. Giant gold dredges operating continuously twenty-four hours a day, creaking and groaning, took chunks of the countryside at a bite, retained the gold ore and discarded the slag, and left behind a strange, useless surrealistic landscape.

Gold mining is no longer an important economic factor around Fairbanks or anywhere in Alaska. The pegged price set in 1944 combined with inflation have decreased both the value and production of gold. Petroleum exploration and development, transportation, tourism, and higher education have replaced it.

Fairbanks is on the Tanana, a branch of the mighty Yukon River, about one hundred twenty miles south of the Arctic Circle. Of our big cities, it is the farthest north. Because it is an administrative, transportation, and supply center for the interior and entire North Slope of Alaska, Fairbanks has a commercial importance beyond its size. Often called the "Golden Heart of Alaska," its trade area is estimated at 227,000 square miles. Both the Alaska Railroad and the Alaska Highway terminate at Fairbanks, which had about twenty thousand inhabitants in 1970. The Tanana Valley is one of the best farming regions in Alaska, especially for cereals, but full advantage has not yet been taken of its agricultural possibilities. Like Anchorage, Fairbanks has an international airport.

The Chena River flows through the center of Fairbanks. In August of 1967 it flooded almost the entire city, producing the worst catastrophe in Fairbanks's history.

The possible hours of sunshine in Fairbanks can vary from four in midwinter to nearly twenty-two in summer. Being far from the ocean and its climatic influences, Alaska's second largest city is generally both colder in winter and hotter in summer than coastal settlements. During the long summer days, which darken to only a bright twilight around midnight, Fairbanks's temperatures frequently rise to 90°F. in the shade —the record is 99°. In winter, as nights grow longer, the cold becomes intense. The thermometer drops to 60° below or lower (the record low is −66°) and the air becomes breathlessly still, for seldom do winds blow at extremely low temperatures, except in the Antarctic. While some activity stops, the railroad continues to run, bringing mail, freight, and passengers; planes arrive and take off—life goes on.

Ice fog, a midwinter phenomenon common to all high Arctic regions, is a real hazard in Fairbanks. It occurs when water vapor is injected into extremely cold air. The water vapor may be naturally produced by animals, people, or industry, and when it meets low temperatures it is frozen into tiny ice crystals. It is similar to fog that occurs elsewhere except that what is water vapor fog in lower latitudes becomes ice fog in higher climes. In Fairbanks ice fog can persist for a week and even ten days, cutting down visibility and making driving and aircraft landings dangerous. The presence of dust and industrial wastes in the air worsens the situation and what is a spontaneous occurrence at −40° occurs now thanks to pollution at −20°. Fairbanks is particularly prone to ice fog because it is surrounded by hills on three sides, and there is little wind to disperse the fog. The problem is compounded by temperature inversions when heavy cold air settles in an area and stays. The

The University of Alaska campus from the air.

lower the temperature, the more numerous the frozen particles and the smaller they are, until, like pollen, they simply float in the air and are almost impossible to dislodge. When temperatures fall below −22°, ice fog warnings are issued like storm bulletins. The Geophysical Institute at the university is working on the problem.

"The University of Alaska, Fairbanks, is one unit of the University of Alaska State System of higher education . . . It serves people of America's largest state through seven community colleges and three university campuses" (University of Alaska Catalogue for 1970–71). It is unique among institutions of higher learning in the United States in that it serves "within the scope of its resources all the public education needs beyond high school of an entire state." Alaska Methodist University in Anchorage with its handsome Edward Durrell Stone buildings set in a wooded campus has recently joined the system, leaving only Sheldon Jackson College at Sitka independent.

The university has an enrollment of about three thousand students at Fairbanks and is the heart of Alaska's intellectual life and researches. Its main campus permits an extraordinarily wide range of scholarly investigation, ranging from scientific stations on floating ice islands in the Polar Sea to the domestication of musk-ox. All the peculiarly northern physical phenomena are present or handily nearby—glaciers, muskeg, permafrost, and aurora borealis. There are human resources, too—Eskimos, Indians, and Aleuts, whose history, folklore, and languages are being studied in depth and taught in new ways. The wildlife, the still relatively unexplored mineral resources, the problems of northern agriculture, and the strange uneven quality of Alaska's economy are all subjects studied by the large number of departments, institutes, and centers related to the university. Many federally funded projects work with and through the university, like the Office of Naval Research's Arctic Research Laboratory in Point Barrow, which is run by the university.

One of the liveliest and most impressive places on the Fairbanks campus is the Geophysical Institute, which had the distinction of being first to spot *Sputnik*, the Russian space satellite that led all the rest. More recently, to inaugurate its handsome new eight-story Elvey Building, a star-studded symposium on polar science was held on campus in June, 1970. Soviet, Japanese, British, Canadian, and U.S. experts dedicated the buildings and pledged a cooperative study of polar phenomena. The Geophysical Institute is staffed by 160 scientists of the highest caliber, some of them world famous. They teach thirty-three graduate students working for their Ph.D. degrees in polar meteorology, glaciology, oceanography, seismology, vulcanology, tectonic physics, rocketry, upper atmosphere and general geophysical problems. A network of ground stations sends rocket-borne instruments to gather information and return it to a dazzling array of automated scientific-data-gathering machinery. There are laboratories for earthquake prediction, argon gas dating, paleomagnetism, and other exotic uses. The students learn by doing and by assisting their professors.

The atmosphere, as throughout the university, is easy, informal, outdoorsy, still retaining a frontier feeling.

An extraordinary number of scholars and scientists constantly streams in and out of the university, summer and winter, as northern science generally widens its boundaries.

The university has a fine museum, greatly augmented as a result of the late Dr. Otto W. Geist's expeditions to Saint Lawrence Island. A pioneer in Alaskan paleonthology, Dr. Geist gathered a famous collection of fossil materials to add to the historical items in the museum.

Strangely enough the gold mining companies were the

The new Geophysical Institute at the university houses many internationally-known scientists as well as graduate students.

An automated laboratory at the Geophysical Institute which records seismic activity from various stations. Information gathered is used in earthquake prediction studies.

richest source of fossil skeleton remains of Alaska's prehistoric beasts. Dredging operations on nearby creeks in and around Fairbanks turned up quantities of bones from animals that roamed the country tens of thousands of years ago. It was Dr. Geist who first realized that this was a "golden" opportunity in a non-metallic sense. He obtained the cooperation of the U.S. Smelting, Refining and Mining Company, the American Museum of Natural History, and the university, to permit him to rescue these important scientific finds. He educated the mining operators to send for him if any promising bit of ancient bone was revealed as they worked. Geist would dash to the spot, excavate the site carefully, and only then would mining continue. Thanks to the perfect deepfreeze qualities of permafrost, centuries-dead mammoths, some with their flesh and hair intact, have been preserved.

Another area where students gain practical as well as theoretical knowledge at the university is in anthropology.

On the university campus a radio telescope is shown here silhouetted against an auroral sky.

Each summer, field trips are made to study Eskimos and other Indians, often with a professor as leader. Archeological work is sometimes done at the same time or on separate expeditions.

A startling archeological find was made in Alaska in 1939 and 1940 by two faculty members, Froelich G. Rainey and Louis Giddings, and by a visiting Danish Eskimo archeologist, Helge Larsen. At Point Hope, a peninsula in northwestern Alaska which juts into the Polar Sea, they discovered the remains of a unique Arctic metropolis. They unearthed a group of eight hundred dwellings arranged in regular avenues which must have housed a population larger than that of pre-war Fairbanks! Point Hope is 130 miles north of the Arctic Circle, beyond 68° north latitude.

The site, called Ipiutak, is thought to have been built well over a thousand years ago. Excavations yielded beautiful ivory carvings, some of them unlike those of any known northern Eskimo or Indian culture. About five hundred skeletons were recovered. In strange tombs, fashioned of logs, skeletons were revealed which stared up at the archeologists with artificial eyeballs carved of ivory and inlaid with huge jet pupils. Before burial the natural eyes had apparently been gouged out and replaced with ivory substitutes. Ivory mouth covers and nose plugs carved to represent bird beaks added to the fantastic appearance of the skulls. Exquisite spiral carvings of walrus ivory, of unknown use, and delicately made and engraved implements were found in the burials. Many designs of the artifacts resembled those produced in North China two or three thousand years ago; others were like carvings of the Ainu peoples in northern Japan and the Amur River natives of Siberia. This was not the culture of a simple people, but of a highly sophisticated, complex group.

Twentieth-century Point Hope, or Tigerak, "the forefinger," as it is known to the Eskimos, supports a population of about three hundred fifty. The question arises as to how such

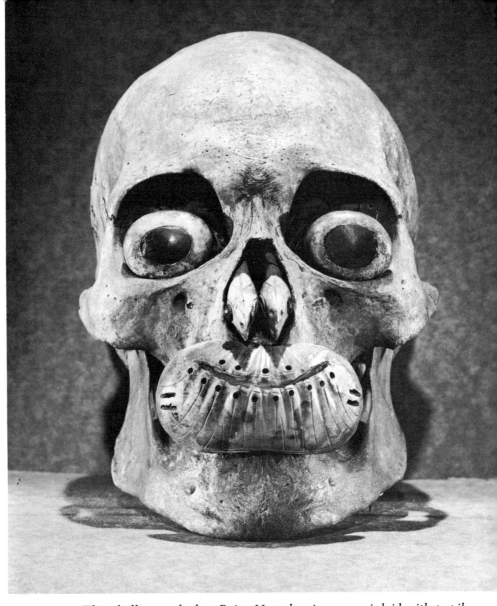

This skull unearthed at Point Hope has ivory eyes inlaid with pupils of jet, and an ivory nose plug and mouth cover.

a large settlement as nearby Ipiutak could have been fed. The answer that comes quickly to mind is the location of Point Hope, directly in the path of the annual northward migration of the bowhead whale. But archeological evidence tells us that Ipiutak people did no whaling but lived on walrus, hair seal, and the huge nine-hundred-pound *ugrug,* or bearded seal.

If they did no whaling, their direct descendants do. Indeed, their lives center around the pursuit of the world's mightiest living mammal. "Leads" are the narrow channels of open water between ice floes. They form close to the land at Point Hope, making both whale and seal hunting relatively easy in winter and spring. The villagers are among the best ice hunters in Alaska. In summer when the ice is gone and land game is scarce the men, like so many other village Eskimos, move to larger villages or to Fairbanks looking for jobs that will bring cash money into the family.

In 1935, back in the days just after the Great Depression, when Alaska was still a territory, 200 families from the relief rolls of several northern states were transported to the Matanuska Valley of Alaska near Palmer to begin a new life. With the help of the federal government, transport was provided, and money loaned for equipment, land purchase, buildings, livestock, and even furniture. By the fall of the next year the farmers' newly built barns were bulging with harvested crops and the new town of Palmer was flourishing. The experiment known as the Matanuska Colony was born in controversy but managed to grow and thrive. With Alaska's increasing population came an increased demand for fresh milk, cream, and vegetables. Combined with Palmer's excellent road, rail, and air connections a prosperous future for the colony seemed assured.

There were 12 farms in Alaska at the beginning of the twentieth century. Their number gradually increased to 639 by 1939, but thereafter improved technology and cheaper, speedier air transportation allowed imported food to compete successfully with locally grown products, and the number of farms declined to 310. The Matanuska Valley around Palmer is still the most important farm area in Alaska, growing 70 percent of the total output. The Tanana Valley, Kenai Peninsula, Southeast and Southwest compete in that order. But only 5 percent of the food eaten in Alaska is grown there. Like

almost everything else in the state, farming is more expensive than in the lower forty-eight. The climate is difficult, the season is short, the cost of labor is high. On the plus side, many insects which plague farmers in warmer climates are absent and the remaining farms are now larger and more productive than formerly. The long summer days limit fiber formation in some vegetables, producing better quality carrots, beets, cabbage, broccoli, and turnips. It is in freezing and exporting these high-quality vegetables that Alaska's successful farming future may lie.

Only a thousand people are engaged in year-round farming

*A farm in the beautiful
Matanuska Valley.*

in Alaska. The eighty dairies that were operating in 1960 followed the farming pattern and were reduced ten years later to thirty-five. The small marginal operation can no longer compete successfully with the larger well-capitalized farm.

As Fairbanks is the market for most of the Tanana Valley farming, so Anchorage, fifty miles away, is Palmer's chief consumer.

Palmer's setting between two dramatic glacier-studded mountain ranges, the Talkeetnas and the Chugachs, makes it a delightful goal for pleasure trips. Sunflowers reaching to the second story of a house and sweet peas ten feet tall with enormous blossoms are common in Palmer and throughout southeastern and south central Alaska. Every familiar flower seems taller, bigger, and brighter than those we are accustomed to in more southerly latitudes.

Long before the coming of the white man, Alaska's salmon provided the prime source of food for Indians living on the coast and inland along rivers. In 1878 the first commercial canneries were established, and within the fifty-year period following, according to Ernest Gruening, Alaska became the world's greatest salmon producer. Salmon surpassed gold min-

ing as the major industry; the salmon industry represented the largest capital investment, showed the biggest annual financial yield, and was the greatest employer of labor. Salmon became the "largest single source of territorial revenue, and the dominant factor in Alaska's political, economic, and social life."

At the end of the 1930s the size of the annual salmon runs for the first time began to decline sharply. Some say overfishing was the cause; others blame insufficient or poorly enforced conservation measures. It seems to have been a complex combination of biological, social, economic, and other forces. Nevertheless the 1968 salmon catch alone was valued at $123

An Indian fishing camp on the Tanana River.

million. During late summer and fall millions of salmon still swim in Alaskan waters on their way to spawn.

That every fish seeks unerringly the river and branch stream of its birth and early development seems so romantic a notion that many have doubted it. Alaskan salmon are known to travel thousands of miles from home, spending the major part of their lives in the world's largest ocean, the Pacific.

Salmon are hatched in fresh water, where they remain two years, and then descend to the sea. When they migrate outbound they are only a few inches long. They grow rapidly in salt water and two or three years later, fully grown, they return each to the stream where it was born, to spawn and die. It is on this homeward migration that the fish are taken for commercial purposes.

Formerly salmon roe was always discarded during processing, but in the 1960s a market was found for it in Japan and now it adds considerably to the value of the salmon catch. Salmon fishing is seasonal, most of it occurring in a single month, even in a two-week period in some areas. The shellfish industry is much less seasonal.

Except for April and May when the crab molt and spawn, crab may be taken all year. The huge, delicious King Crab became extremely popular until it was overfished. As its production declined, Tanner Crab, scallops, and shrimp increased to take its place. Most of the salmon is canned, most of the shellfish is frozen. Alaska still leads all the other states in the value of its fisheries.

Ketchikan, the southernmost good-sized city in Alaska, has been described as three blocks wide and three miles long. One approaches it by ship through islands of green forest, gliding along mirror-still waters. It is a major port of entry and a growing industrial center.

Strung out thinly along a narrow strip of land at the foot of sharply rising Deer Mountain, Ketchikan seems in imminent danger of tumbling into the waters of Tongass Narrows. Every square inch of the crowded city has been utilized and when new streets are needed it is said that they must be blasted out of the solid rock.

A giant new pulp mill, one of the largest in the world, is in Ketchikan. It is a relatively new year-round industry for Alaska and employs a thousand people, half in town and half in the woods. Timber for the mill is cut from the Tongass National Forest's 16 million acres of virgin timber, which occupy most of southeastern Alaska. All cutting is under the strict supervision of the U. S. Forest Service. Other pulp mills in Alaska are at Sitka, Haines, Juneau, and Wrangell.

Ketchikan has skyscraper apartment buildings, modern schools, and attractive new housing developments. The seven thousand people who live there enjoy the cool summers which resemble those of the Maine coast. There is little snowfall in winter, but in all seasons there is rain, rain, and more rain. The abundant rainfall is responsible for ideal tree growing conditions in the area and also for the famous Ketchikan flower gardens. Delphiniums reach eight or nine feet, pansies grow as big as saucers. Although no road connects Ketchikan with other towns, the streets are crowded with automobiles. The city is in touch with the rest of Alaska and "outside" through shipping, the Alaska Marine Highway system, and numerous daily flights. A new multi-million dollar airport is under construction and should be completed in 1973.

Alaska's Farthest North

A glance at a polar projection map of the Northern Hemisphere, or better, at the top of a globe, shows the countries of the North grouped around a smallish sea called the Arctic Ocean; more accurately, it is a Polar Mediterranean. As the Old World Mediterranean lies between Europe and Africa, so

Ketchikan is strung out along a narrow strip of land at the foot of Deer Mountain. Note the fishing boats in the harbor.

the northernmost body of water, surrounded by the powerful nations of the world, lies between North America with Greenland, Canada, and Alaska on one side, and northern Europe and Asia on the other.

On the shores of the Polar Mediterranean the most northerly cape in our most northerly state is Point Barrow. As the planes fly it is five hundred miles northeast of Nome and the same distance northwest of Fairbanks. Its Eskimo name is Nuwuk, meaning "the point." Our name for it dates from 1826 when Captain Beechey named it after Sir John Barrow, the great British patron of Arctic exploration who was responsible for his Parliament's offering a twenty thousand pound reward to the first navigator of the Northwest Passage.

About nine miles southwest of Point Barrow is the village of Barrow. It was here that a trading post was first established in 1885 by the later famous Charles D. Brower. The post is still flourishing, although Charlie is gone now and his son Tom runs it. Charlie Brower played host to many famous explorers in the more than fifty years he lived in Barrow. Will Rogers and Wiley Post were on their way to visit him when their plane crashed and they lost their lives. In his book, *Fifty Years Below Zero*, Brower gives the highlights of his long and interesting life. Tom Brower continues the family tradition as an unofficial greeter and influential citizen.

Nowadays a great many more people turn up at Barrow than ever did in his father's day. Barrow's population (2,104 in 1970) has doubled since 1950 and it now has the largest Eskimo settlement in the United States. Its growth is mainly due to the employment opportunities offered by a constellation of federal government departments, the Bureau of Indian Affairs office, the U.S. Public Health Service fourteen-bed hospital, and the Office of Naval Research's Arctic Research Laboratory.

NARL, established in 1947 in a quonset hut of the Naval Petroleum Reserve No. 4 not far from Barrow, is the only U.S.

scientific station devoted entirely to Arctic basic research. When the navy finished its oil exploration in the area the Lab inherited the quonset hut village left behind. It has now grown to have a permanent staff of about one hundred. There is always another hundred visiting scientists and researchers from universities and other government departments who come for long or short periods depending on the type of investigation they are pursuing. Owned by the navy, it is run by contract with the University of Alaska through a civilian administrator, presently John Schindler. Its research projects cover a geographical area stretching from Bering Strait to Greenland and including the Polar Sea. It has its own fleet of half a dozen specially equipped aircraft, tracked vessels, motor-driven sleds, and other vehicles needed to support researchers working in-

An aerial view of the NARL Laboratory in 1968.

Wolves, along with many other Arctic animals, are maintained in the NARL Zoo for scientific study.

land, along the coast, out on the sea ice, or in the air. It has its own research library, museum, and private zoo whose tenants vary from year to year but usually include polar bears, wolves, wolverines, snowy owls, and other animals interesting to biologists and physiologists. In addition to the quonset hut village, NARL has a remarkable permanent building completed in 1968 which is probably the most modern architectural complex in our Far North. To prevent the heat of the buildings from thawing the permafrost below, the building is mounted on 557 piles sunk fifteen feet into the frozen ground with an air space left between ground and building. Its seven wings house forty-one separate modern laboratories for performing every imaginable kind of research, as well as attractive living quarters and common rooms for staff and visitors, painted in many different colors.

It is from this center of Arctic learning that the famous ice island floating scientific stations in the Polar Sea are staffed and supported. Drifting laboratories like T-3 (Fletcher's Ice Island) and ARLIS II (Arctic Research Laboratory Ice Station No. 2) are a wonderful means of obtaining scientific information about what is happening above, below, and in the sea ice in areas where ships cannot operate without the gravest danger, if at all, because of the ice.

The Lab even has an important role in the local whaling operations, which continue to be an important food source for the local Eskimos, as well as those at Point Hope, Wainwright, and Gambell. It is now from radio monitors placed by NARL that the first warning of an approaching whale comes. This year (1972) when the offshore lead opened on April 20, whaling

Max Brewer, the first director of NARL, with two young Arctic wolverines, ages five weeks (foreground) and nine weeks.

began, and by May 3 Barrow had gotten thirteen whales, which meant meat and muktuk for all.

A well in its own back yard supplies the Laboratory with natural gas and a special law permits it to be sold locally to Barrow citizens at cost.

Long- and short-term scientific programs in oceanography, geology, geophysics, sea ice, permafrost, underwater accoustics, northern biology, adaptations of man and animals to cold, and many other areas are conducted from the Lab. Despite the difficult climate, the absence of roads, problems of permafrost, and flights cancelled because of weather, the NARL is a cheerful busy place. Scientists, technicians, and secretaries in an atmosphere of cheery purposefulness are all "doing their thing" and providing the rest of us with the knowledge we need to operate at greater efficiency in the Far North while safeguarding the ecological balance.

An innovation of recent years at Barrow is the tourist business. In summer extra flights bring vacationers from many parts of the continent—people who want to set foot on the northernmost tip of Alaska, see how the Eskimos live, and perhaps have a ride in a skin-covered umiak. For Barrow Eskimos, although most of them receive high wages working six days a week for the government, still hunt walrus and whale as their ancestors did. The Top of the World Hotel at Point Barrow, owned and operated by Eskimos, accommodates visitors. If the weather is nippy, and it usually is here even in summer, fur-trimmed parkas are supplied by the airline hostesses.

Further tourist entertainment is provided of a summer evening at the Eskimo Dance House. Here to the accompaniment of high-pitched singing and the hypnotic sound of a dozen drums beating complicated rhythms in perfect unison, Eskimo dances are performed in full costume. While tourists make up the larger part of the audience, they are joined by middle-aged and older local residents who love to hear the old

*Drum dance at Barrow. Eskimos formerly had no word of greeting.
Now* koyanuk, *which means "excellent," is used in many areas.*

songs and see the traditional dances. The younger set seems to
prefer rock-and-roll dancing down the street a bit, to the strains
of the juke box. Young dancers turn and twist as they expertly
perform their complicated steps. At a distance they look like
any group of teen-agers performing the same ritual in more
southerly places.

Barrow is in truly Arctic country. More than three hundred
miles north of the Arctic Circle, it is far from any warm
currents like those of the Gulf Stream that bathe the northern
coasts of Norway in similar latitudes. Here great masses of ice,
pressed forward by wind and current, grind against the shore
in winter, producing the heaviest ice pack known in any part

of the world. There is permafrost here; only from about six to eighteen inches of the earth's surface thaws downward in summer. Because of the permafrost below, the hot sun above, and the absence of sidewalks, the streets are muddy, and boots, whether rubber or sealskin, are a must. The frost below the surface which creates so many building problems, happily provides free refrigeration for food storage chambers dug into frozen soil. Meat has been kept fresh for years in these natural deepfreezes. Where the vegetation is undisturbed, the meadows are covered with rich grass.

As in all other towns in the permafrost zone of Alaska, water for drinking, cooking, and bathing presents a problem. In Point Barrow and similar towns, water must be hauled, often from great distances, and is sold by the drum, making bathing an expensive luxury. At Barrow water is now three dollars per fifty-five-gallon drum in summer and thirty-five cents per cubic foot of ice in winter. Water for laundry and cleaning purposes must also be purchased, increasing the already fearfully high cost of living. But if the cost of living is high, so are wages.

A worldwide problem that has accompanied the population explosion is the disposal of human wastes, trash, garbage, and sewage. In a place like Barrow the problem is compounded because permafrost prevents any underground sewage disposal, and cold above ground makes natural decay incredibly slow. Early explorers used to report with surprise finding tracks of vehicles, wood chips, and campfire remnants, which looked as though they had just been made, but had actually been made a century before. For thousands of years the Eskimos occupied the surrounding areas leaving so few traces of their passage that it takes a trained archeologist to detect their camping places. Modern man with his oversupply of plastic, paper, and metal containers and his inability to think of others has left scenes of the most horrible disorder all over the Arctic (as well as in lower latitudes). This year (1972) the navy will spend $1.5

million cleaning up the mess they left behind years ago at the Naval Petroleum Reserve.

The Eskimos, who have picked up many of our bad habits, have recently taken over one more. Living as we do in one place, buying our kind of canned and packaged foods in the local store, they too now have ugly little dump heaps outside the back of their houses.

It is ironic that Barrow, which has had closed-circuit TV for some years and a relatively rich cash economy, still doesn't have a high school. Barrow Eskimos must leave home if they want to go on with their education after grade school. At long last, however, a regional high school is under way for five hundred students and is expected to be finished in 1976. It will be very modern and include kitchen facilities, gym, and, a genuine innovation for Barrow youngsters, a swimming pool!

The tip of our northernmost sandspit is not the boundary marking the end of all activity. Yankee whalers learned a century ago that fortunes could be built in Massachusetts on whalebone from the sea beyond the coast. Stefansson proved on his 1913–18 sledge journeys over the ice that life in the sea does not cease beyond where ships are able to penetrate. His party lived by hunting seals as they traveled afoot over the moving pack ice many hundreds of miles north of Alaskan land. Later Papanin and his colleagues demonstrated, in 1937, that the waters of the Polar Mediterranean are teeming with animal and plant life even at the very North Pole, more than a thousand miles north of Barrow. Recently there have been many scientific stations set down on ice islands in the polar pack, both by the Soviets and by us.

In August of 1958 the nuclear-powered submarine *Nautilus* completed a passage under the pack ice, from Bering Strait to the North Pole, emerging in the Greenland Sea north of Iceland. Her sister ship, the *Skate,* soon afterward made the same magnificent journey in the opposite direction, surfacing through the ice at the North Pole. Three hundred miles to the

The shore lead off Point Barrow where the migrating whales pass. Two whaling camps are visible on the horizon.

south, on the Alaska side, they surfaced again to greet and visit with the scientists on the drifting ice station *Alpha*, engaged in International Geophysical Year investigations.

In the Arctic, the North Pole is the center of a deep, liquid sea. This is exactly opposite to the Antarctic, where the South Pole is the center of a huge ice-covered continent. A surprising number of people still hold the erroneous belief, which dates back to classic Greek times, that the Arctic Sea is frozen to the bottom. Another misconception was encouraged by almost every newspaper and magazine reporting the *Nautilus* voyage, stating that the submarine traveled below the "icecap under the North Pole." There is no icecap at, under, or anywhere near the North Pole. By definition, an icecap is a large, land-based glacier composed of fresh ice, which in earlier times was newly fallen snow. The relatively thin, fractured shell of ice which floats on our northernmost sea is salt water ice, which has a different composition, freezing point, color, texture and behavior under pressure or melting, than fresh ice. Sea ice may range in thickness from fractions of an inch to a maximum thickness of eleven to thirteen feet.

Arctic Sea ice would resemble a thin, smooth shell, were it not for winds and currents. Winds, however gentle, and currents, however sluggish, are sufficient to break the cover into ice floes of every imaginable shape and size and to keep them constantly on the move. In winter they move rather slowly; in summer they move somewhat more freely, the spaces between floes widening to reveal more patches of blue, open water. In midsummer as much as 25 percent of the Polar Sea may be open water where whales and submarines alike may surface with ease.

Winds and currents which break the ice cover are also responsible for grinding the floes against each other at their edges, or piling them up into pressure ridges against the land-fast shore ice, where it meets the moving pack. These pressure ridges, startling and dramatic in size and shape, are seldom higher above water than one hundred feet. Two hundred feet therefore is about the maximum thickness of sea ice above and below water. For a pressure ridge, if you visualize the whole of it, is usually pyramid-shaped, the base of the pyramid below water level.

Another misconception about the Arctic Sea is that it is filled with innumerable icebergs. Practically speaking, there are no icebergs in the Arctic Sea. Greenland, our greatest northern iceberg factory, discharges its bergs to the east and west, but all are borne southward by the prevailing currents and eventually they die in the warm waters of the North Atlantic. All icebergs were once part of a glacier and their ice is therefore fresh. When a glacier extends down to the sea and out over the water, it is the floating section that breaks off to become an iceberg, and the birth process is called *calving*.

To further complicate the differences between salt and fresh ice, salt sea ice when it is sufficiently old, becomes fresh. In alternate freezing and thawing that occurs with the changing season, the salt content of sea ice migrates toward whichever side is warmer, usually downward, and the briny particles are eventually eliminated. When sea ice is more than two years old its melt water can be used for drinking. After three years, no saltiness in floating sea ice can be detected except by delicate chemical test—the human palate cannot detect it. This has been known for centuries by the practical sealers and whalers who wintered often in the North.

Thanks to the drifting ice stations we now know the path of the Arctic Ocean drifts. Oceanographers have charted the mountains and valleys of the undersea landscape and can tell their age and provenance. Marine biologists have described the live inhabitants of the cold, salty water and the astonishing activity of tiny creatures on the underside of the pack ice. Physicists explain the crystalline structure of the sea ice. Zoologists have studied and listed the animals which walk on and fly over the ice. Still others measure and record aspects of the climate as far as rockets will go. On the land similar investigations have wiped out innumerable blank spots in our knowledge.

Our little world has been entirely discovered and we must close the book of primary exploration and open two others. The first is that of outer space and the universe as a whole. The geography of Mars and the moon is no longer a matter for speculation. The second is the exploration of ways and means of preserving and improving our decaying, polluted, over-populated spaceship earth.

Just as we now know how to build on permafrost without deforming the land and how to travel in the Arctic without destroying the fragile ecosystem, the knowledge of how to preserve our planet has accumulated. The looming question of more importance to our children than to us is—will we use it?

Index